T0271436

Developing Age-Friendly Communities in the UK

The ageing population is a global societal issue. Policymakers, planners and the public, third and private sectors must rethink how the built environment and services are delivered to meet the needs of a changing demographic. This is the first book to systematically review the evolution, development and progress of age-friendly thinking in the UK, with a primary focus on the real-world experiences of the people leading place-based initiatives.

The book presents the findings of the first in-depth national study of age-friendly programme leaders in the UK, completed in 2021, and provides insights into the development of age-friendly communities, the formative influences from a social policy perspective, the management challenges and the progress towards achieving age-friendly goals. Using primary interview data and narrative analysis, the experiences of working with age-friendly programmes in different organisational forms are explored.

The book promotes a greater understanding of what it means to become an age-friendly community in practice, how the programmes have different development pathways, and what influences different outcomes. Embellished with detailed narratives from practitioners, informative tables, and diagrams and figures throughout, the book carefully gathers the voices of a diverse range of decision-makers and leaders associated with the age-friendly movement and provides unique insights on the drivers of change in specific localities. This is a must-read for anyone involved in ageing research or ageing policy and practice as it provides an insightful look into the real world of embedding this community development model in different localities to make a difference to the lives of older people. Topical themes include how these agendas connect with other issues, such as dementia-friendly programmes and the work of the third sector, as well as the growing challenge of what it means to be 'friendly' as a community and place and whether 'friendly' is becoming an over-used term in relation to place identity.

The book has national and global interest for all communities engaged in age-friendly activity, offering exemplars of best practice, achievements in transforming local communities and views on the meaning of ageing, as well as the age-friendly lens as an approach that champions the world through the eyes of older people. It offers a thought-provoking read for anyone with an interest in this expanding area of ageing, irrespective of disciplinary focus.

Stephen J. Page is Associate Dean (Research) at Hertfordshire Business School, University of Hertfordshire, and Professor of Business and Management, Hatfield, UK.

Joanne Connell is Associate Professor in Sustainability and Tourism at the University of Exeter Business School, Exeter, UK.

Developing Age-Friendly Communities in the UK
Re-creating Places and Spaces

Stephen J. Page and Joanne Connell

Routledge
Taylor & Francis Group

LONDON AND NEW YORK

First published 2023
by Routledge
4 Park Square, Milton Park, Abingdon, Oxon OX14 4RN

and by Routledge
605 Third Avenue, New York, NY 10158

Routledge is an imprint of the Taylor & Francis Group, an informa business

© 2023 Stephen J. Page and Joanne Connell

British Library Cataloguing-in-Publication Data
A catalogue record for this book is available from the British Library

Library of Congress Cataloging-in-Publication Data
Names: Page, Stephen, 1963– author. | Connell, Joanne, author.
Title: Developing age friendly communities in the UK : re-creating places and spaces / Stephen J. Page and Joanne Connell.
Description: Abingdon, Oxon ; New York, NY : Routledge, 2023. | Includes bibliographical references and index.
Subjects: LCSH: Aging—Social aspects—Great Britain. | Older people—Great Britain—Social conditions. | Older people—Services for—Great Britain. | Community development—Great Britain. | City planning—Great Britain.
Classification: LCC HQ1064.G7 P34 2023 (print) | LCC HQ1064.G7 (ebook) | DDC 305.260941—dc23/eng/20220729
LC record available at https://lccn.loc.gov/2022028646
LC ebook record available at https://lccn.loc.gov/2022028647

ISBN: 978-1-032-33478-3 (hbk)
ISBN: 978-1-032-33479-0 (pbk)
ISBN: 978-1-003-31980-1 (ebk)

DOI: 10.4324/9781003319801

Typeset in Times New Roman
by Apex CoVantage, LLC

Contents

Plates

Figures

Tables

Acknowledgements

The authors would like to express their sincere thanks to the participants from the UK Network of Age-Friendly Communities for the very generous amount of time they provided in discussing the age-friendly programme in the UK and how it applied in their localities. We hope they will find the book of value in providing the first systematic national synthesis of their work based on the interviews they provided. Stephen would also like to thank the Hertfordshire Business School for a period of sabbatical leave in 2021 to undertake the interviews along with financial support towards the transcription of the interviews and the costs associated with producing this research monograph. In addition, thanks go to Emma Travis for supporting the project and Harriet Cunningham for handling its administrative aspects.

1 Introduction

Introduction: Ageing as a societal issue

The world's population is ageing: that is a truism. As the United Nations Department of Economic and Social Affairs (2019) indicates, the world's population will continue to transition from a position where in 2019 1:11 people were aged over 65 (9% of the total population) to a ratio of 1:6 by 2050 (16% of the total population). In some regions such as North America and Europe this ratio of people aged over 65 to those under 65 will rise to 1:4 by 2050. In 2018 the number of people aged over 65 outnumbered the number of children under five years of age globally. The consequence of this major demographic shift is that by 2050, the number of those aged 80 years or over will have tripled, from 143 million in 2019 to 426 million (United Nations Department of Economic and Social Affairs 2019). The literature on ageing does not necessarily agree on the point at which a population ages, as human ageing begins at the point of birth. Old age is a complex term, as the period of old age may begin in middle age and extend for up to half of an adult's overall life course. During this time, they may transition through the following stages of ageing: independence, interdependence, dependency, crisis management and finally the end of life. Therefore, if we are seeking a point at which old age begins, various definitions and categorisations suggest it might start in the range of 55–65 years of age. The 60–65 age category is used frequently by governments to identify the starting point for pensions and benefits related to old age. Some studies also point to ageing being a perceptual issue – it is in the eye of the beholder and is related to individual capabilities and life history as well as the factors that impact on health and well-being (see Patterson 2018 for more detail). In many studies, organisations such as the United Nations World Health Organization have adopted the age of 60 as a starting point for old age, although there is no agreed definition. It is perhaps more important for a study of age-friendliness to adopt a more fluid definition that recognises the needs of an ageing population in terms of accessibility and encourages

DOI: 10.4324/9781003319801-1

their greater participation in society. It is also worth noting that many of the issues around ageing seem to emerge within the population after age 55, although official classifications of ageing tend to adopt calendar age as the main criteria regardless of ability and need.

The nature of the demographic shift in the age structure of global and national populations has been known for many decades. Conversely, this demographic shift has assumed a very low priority for many governments, largely because of the enormity of the changes and adaptations it will require in every aspect of life, work and society. For many governments, it has been convenient, for reasons of short-term political expediency, to commission reports and inquiries and defer decisions on the policy changes to later governments. In one respect, this is perhaps explained by the major shift in thinking required by the state and its organisations to tackle the multifaceted issue of ageing, which transcends the remit of many government departments and bodies. Critics have pointed to the universal failure of many governments' social policies to broach the radical changes that an ageing demographic will require in terms of service delivery, infrastructure provision and the scale of financial resources needed to adapt and develop a more age-aware society. For too long, ageing has been seen as a background issue in many countries as it is not perceived as a net generator of taxation and income or as a consistently newsworthy item, like climate change. Instead, it is seen as a resource-consumptive issue that crosscuts every area of life, including communities, the economy and the environment.

Despite a lack of political action on ageing (aside from periodic government reviews and inquiries), it has developed as a popular theme for discussion in the social sciences, sciences, medicine and popular media over the last 100 years. The scientific development of gerontology is one marker of that interest in ageing, which can be dated to the 1950s (e.g. Shock 1952). Shock (1952: 1) explained that gerontology '. . . is the scientific study of the phenomenon of ageing . . . [and that] . . . the problems of gerontology are multidimensional and will require for their solution not only a multidisciplinary approach but also a correlation of diverse finding and viewpoints'. Shock recognised the multifaceted nature of ageing as a societal issue, and this provided a counterbalance to the medical interest in ageing. The rise of geriatric medicine as a sub-specialism in medicine is often attributed to its foundation in London in the 1930s (Ritch 2012). The focus of geriatric medicine is often described as being preoccupied with the five geriatric giants – iatrogenesis (a state of ill health caused unintentionally by medical care such as misdiagnosis, adverse drug reactions or infections caused by inadequate hygiene by healthcare workers), immobility, instability, incontinence and impaired cognition (Greenstein et al. 2019). Popular media tends to seize upon very emotive issues around ageing, from loneliness or service failure in social care to the hidden army of unpaid carers looking after elderly relatives living at home, and the low pay of social carers. The importance of media forays into ageing issues tends to reiterate the critical realignment needed in welfare systems, which in some cases are over 100 years old, and were built upon philosophical principles that never foresaw universal care for the scale of the ageing population facing many countries. In other settings, that principle of universal care is the natural corollary of a central state policy towards ageing by more forward-thinking governments. Whilst philosophical transformations in social policy, which we examine below, have meant that welfarism has created a greater universality of care for the population per se, radical policy analyses suggest that the universality principles of welfarism may need to be rethought and revised given the financial challenge ageing will pose for future government finances. In short, the Victorian principles of self-help, self-reliance and the unpopular principle (in those times) of less eligibility, which will also be examined later in this chapter, are likely to resurface in uncomfortable policy debates on how to meet the needs of an ageing population. From a critical perspective, the pursuit of age-friendly policies may be interpreted as an attempt by the local state to address its responsibility for the ageing population in the absence of central state policies towards that population, where there is a policy vacuum. Thus, age-friendly thinking is an important part of the process of change needed to transform our society to accommodate ageing. Yet the theoretical interpretations and approaches we might adopt to interpret these changes are potentially diverse, as are the disciplines and political viewpoints that contribute to its meaning, development and implementation.

Approaches towards ageing as a social phenomenon span a continuum, with two broadly opposing views: a pessimistic and a more positive approach. The pessimistic view of ageing is rooted in the concept of the life course (Harper 2006) and the human inevitability of ageing that poses challenges for individuals, illustrated by the initial scope of geriatric medicine. Studies, such as Nair (2005), outline the scope of the enhanced risks associated with ageing, including trips, slips, falls, fire, hospitalisation, impairment, and risks with driving, travel, and flying. As a consequence, a proportion of the older population becomes confined to residential care due to ongoing health and care needs as vulnerable citizens. This pessimistic view has been a dominant way of thinking about ageing based on empirical validation of physical processes of ageing, even though such processes of ageing affects people in different ways. Furthermore, it aligns with the role of the state as a primary welfare provider in meeting the basic human needs of a more vulnerable population. Other, more positive approaches are illustrated by an interest in keeping the ageing population healthier for longer, premised on meeting the basic human right to live and participate in a civil society. The arguments from a positive viewpoint move us from a more minimalist state intervention position of dealing with humane crises (e.g. health, shelter and hunger), to consider how we can enable ageing people to realise the potential of a new phase of life, and to enjoy fulfilling and rewarding lives. An enabling role may mean that restrictive barriers to participation (e.g. the built environment and services) must be addressed. The positive view of ageing informs much of the thinking we explore in this book in order to understand the changes needed to achieve a more age-friendly society at a community or place-specific level in recreating place and space for later life. Our focus is perceived as enabling the normalisation of ageing, whilst recognising that older people are faced with barriers and obstacles that arise because of their stage in their life course.

There are many disciplinary perspectives we could adopt to approach this topic, but in the case of age-friendly initiatives and their implementation, we must recognise that much of the responsibility for this rests with the public sector in most countries (although the private sector also has a key role to play, when facilitated by the public sector). For this reason, the initial theoretical framework that has shaped the development and implementation of age-friendly initiatives is rooted in social policy, to which our attention now turns. This does not mean other perspectives are not equally important, as we shall examine in Chapter 2, but our initial starting point for an examination of 'age-friendly' as a concept begins with a reflective and historical narrative on social policy and ageing in the UK, to identify how the concept of age-friendly marks a significant step change in thinking about ageing.

Social policy and ageing: Historical antecedents

Social policy in its broadest sense is concerned with human needs, how society meets those needs (e.g. the needs of its ageing citizens) and how the state allocates resources to address them. It can also embrace how the state seeks to address societal problems, including how the welfare state (where one exists) seeks to meet basic human needs such as shelter, food, heat, water, health and education, to enable those citizens to participate in society. Consequently, issues such as inequality, poverty, access to resources and social justice and how the state delivers services to meet human needs have been the focus of social policy analysis. The field of social policy is inherently interdisciplinary, cross-cutting many of the themes which the public sector addresses and that affect human well-being. Within the social sciences, social policy emerged as a subject of academic endeavour in the post-war period in parallel with the emergence of welfare policies in many countries to enhance the standard of welfare provision for their population.

Whilst social policy research studies the causes of societal problems, many explanations for these look at the inequalities which a capitalist society produces through the unequal distribution of resources. Some university departments have been studying societal issues for over a century. For example, the London School of Economics Department of Social Policy was established in 1912. Its socialist ideals were at the heart of its foundation, adding to its research interest in social policy and the analysis of the multifaceted nature of social problems in an urban industrial society. The development of social policy analysis is often attributed to the formative studies of Titmuss (1951). Titmuss' focus was on public administration, a subject area that further developed into social policy, as studies such as Thane (1978, 1989) illustrate in terms of the emergence of the welfare state in the UK.

Social policy as a formative area of research has its roots in the analysis of societal issues in the Victorian and Edwardian periods, which emanated from the social problems that were being caused by rapid industrialisation and urbanisation in a capitalist society (Hobsbawm 2010; Powell 1996), including the creation of an underclass (e.g. Stedman-Jones 1971). One of the dominant areas of analysis throughout the Victorian and Edwardian eras was the focus on poverty, and the analysis of old age in terms of the state policies towards poverty delivered by the new Poor Law with its principle of *less eligibility*, which meant that state support was designed to be the last resort and the least attractive option (see Rose 1985). In contrast, other tenets of modern-day social work and social policy development can be seen as having their roots in the work of charitable bodies such as the Charity Organisation Society (COS, founded 1869; Mowat 1957, 1961) with its concern with poverty and destitution and its use of casework (which predates and was a precursor to its use in modern-day social work). The COS examined the family life course, family history and life events in shaping family circumstances and experiences of poverty and destitution, particularly those occurring in old age (Page 1988). The COS' social caseworker collected the information and recorded it in case histories in considerable detail (see Page 1987), and then a committee determined whether families and individuals were *deserving* or *undeserving* of charitable relief, with a narrative on the rationale. Social surveys of the poor by Booth (1889) and Rowntree (1901) adopted a similar empirical household approach that recognised how old age was a major contributor to poverty in relation to the life course (Page 1988). Ageing was an implicit concern because of the lack of any state safety net beyond the extremities of Poor Law provision via the despised workhouse system, or its outdoor relief system for assisting people who were not destitute, which was delivered alongside charitable provision. *But why is this historical perspective relevant for the analysis of ageing and social policy?*

A historical perspective demonstrates that ageing is not a new theme in social policy terms and that many of the issues which have preoccupied researchers remain as relevant today as they were in the Victorian period. Thomson (1984) concluded that the welfare state has not adapted to the demographic challenge presented by the elderly since the introduction of the New Poor Law in 1834, especially in its failure to pay adequate state pensions to most of the population, as it was 'accepted in the present century that the elderly should be given little more than one-third of the resources of other adults' (Thomson 1984: 453). Taking a historical perspective gives us an important opportunity to reflect on how social policy towards ageing has evolved – particularly in its growing preoccupation with social care – and how policy shifts in the last 200 years have redefined how the ageing agenda is addressed by the state, as well as contextualising how this book fits into these evolving agendas. Jones (2007) provides one of the most succinct overviews of how social policy in the post-war period towards older people in society, delivered as social care in the UK, evolved with the changing philosophies and practices as regards ageing people. Jones suggested that a continuum of social care approaches has developed, from being initially focused on doing 'to' people (with a controlling and containing approach to caring for people institutionally); to doing 'for' them (comprising a paternalistic approach to looking after people); to doing 'with' them (comprising partnerships and participation); and finally, an approach emphasising 'independence and choice', so that people can live independent lives. As Jones (2007) argued, a realisation of the state costs associated with institutionalisation of care after 1989, with residential care costs expanding and increasing the burden on adult social service departments, and a further shift after 2005 towards a well-being focus saw the local state role move from the role of care provider to planning and purchasing care options. Jones (2007) concluded that the future direction for ageing will need to move away from the still-existing principles of less eligibility, established by the Poor Law, to either a rights-based approach to entitlements or a more radical approach that is based on universal service provision for an ageing population.

The antecedents of these approaches to ageing were partly shaped by the early roots of the welfare state, which can be found in social policies developed in the reforming Edwardian Liberal government of 1906–11. One policy innovation was the introduction of old-age pensions (for those over 70) and the ready acceptance of the role of charity in supplementing state resources. Studies such as Booth (1894) found that poverty and old age were interconnected, as 29% of old people (defined as people over the age of 65) received either indoor relief in a workhouse (8.5%) or outdoor relief (19%). Rowntree (1901) observed that an inability to work in older age meant that poverty was the inevitable outcome for many ageing people, even where pension provisions from trade unions and friendly societies existed, as these were too limited to last into older age. In other words, the notion of old age and state dependency was well established in these and subsequent studies (also see Walker 1980).

The 1895 Royal Commission on the Aged Poor examined evidence that demonstrated that outdoor relief was inadequate for the ageing poor, irrespective of the moral arguments that existed at the time on the *deserving* and *undeserving poor*. Booth's (1894) study, alongside the 1895 Royal Commission, provided an impetus for the creation of old-age pensions (Boyer and Schmidle 2009) as the following evidence from Booth's research, reanalysed by Boyer and Schmidle, was indicative of the ageing problem: The life expectancy of those who had reached age 65 in 1901 was around an extra 10 years of life, and the inadequacy of their pension savings meant a reliance upon the Poor Law. This was reflected in the 17–29% of workhouse inmates nationally who were aged over 65, with workhouses accounting for around 30% of all relief provided; the remaining 70% was outdoor relief. Critiques of the Royal Commission reports reaffirmed the link between old age and poverty (Yule 1899; also see Hepple 2001) since 'incapacity for work resulting from old age' (Royal Commission on the Aged Poor 1895: vi) challenged the Victorian ideology of Smiles (Smiles 1859) of *self-reliance*. Self-reliance was the antithesis of state dependency on the Poor Law regardless of its cause, with industriousness and hard work deemed the solution to poverty. The exception was where membership of friendly societies helped with the three 'temporal contingencies in life' (illness, unemployment and death). Further philosophical developments that challenged these idioms included the *common good* concept, articulated in the idealism arguments of T. H. Green, which influenced the thinking behind the liberal reforms of the Edwardian period (Simhony 2005). These ideas were complemented by Hobhouse's (1911) *Liberalism*, which was interpreted as one of the early examples of social liberalism because it reinforced the importance of Green's common good and argued for the importance of showing greater social responsibility towards others, as 'the life of society is rightly held to be organic, and all considered public policy must be conceived in its bearing on the life of society as a whole' (Hobhouse 1911: 74). Hobhouse's concept of an organic society conveys the mutually dependent nature of the individual and society. Herein lies the philosophical basis of the case for a positive view of ageing and the need for the state to recognise its responsibility to others in society, especially those in old age, a time when pressures such as illness, poverty and barriers to participation in society emerge. As Richter (1964: 1) argued in the case of T. H. Green, 'few if any other philosophers exerted a greater influence upon British thought and public policy'. The idea of a collective responsibility to help those less fortunate in society, such as the ageing and infirm, also sparked a major growth in Victorian philanthropy in the mid-to-late Victorian period; this would seed the later acceptance of the new liberalism of the Edwardian period, which embraced greater state responsibility for the social well-being of the population. Green's ideas were juxtaposed with some middle-class thinking that was still wedded to the Smilesean ideology supporting a sense of individualism, although Green argued that individual freedom and personal fulfilment could only be attained through the efforts of society. Again, the idea that personal freedom can only be achieved in relation to ageing by removal of the barriers to participation, so as to reach the state of self-fulfilment, is a central facet of this thinking.

A further Royal Commission report in 1905 on the Poor Law observed that its provision was wholly inadequate for the needs of the aged poor (see Plate 1.1), especially the availability of medical treatment (Royal Commission on the Poor Laws and Relief of Distress, 1905–9). Although measures such as the Old Age Pension Act (1908) resulted in the provision of state pensions for almost 400,000 people over 70 years of age in 1909, these still only covered 37% of all over 70-year-olds (Plate 1.2). Even with the reform of the Poor Law in 1929 and 1948, when the UK National Health system replaced workhouse care for the elderly, ageing remained a background issue with former workhouses often converted to become geriatric (and general) hospitals, a practice that persisted up until the 1970s, or longer in some cases. The shift towards care homes emerged as a solution for those elderly who required constant care.

Much of the optimism that surrounded the post-war welfare state in the UK was not fulfilled in terms of the way the ageing population would be viewed or treated in a post-war society. Townsend's (1981) analysis of the social policy towards ageing in the UK in the post-war period challenged the entire basis of social policy as meeting the needs of the aged as: 'society creates the framework of institutions and rules within which the problems of the elderly emerge, and indeed, are manufactured' (Townsend 1981: 9). Townsend highlighted the continued institutionalisation of the ageing population. He recognised that the state's institutionalised approach to ageing, particularly towards poverty and old age, was very much at odds with the welfare state's objectives. Some critics have gone as far as to suggest that the post-war period in the UK is characterised by a dearth of social policy towards ageing per se, with most policies targeted at specific problem areas associated with institutional care and housing rather than a broader concern for the well-being of, and provision for, an increasingly ageing society. Whilst a micro-level policy analysis of individual state policies would certainly challenge this argument if we consider the piecemeal changes made in some areas of government social policy, there has been no overarching thinking on ageing at a state level consistent with the post-war ideals of the welfare state (The Joseph Rowntree Foundation Task Group on Housing, Money and Care For Older People 2004). It is only comparatively recently that the political focus has shifted towards the need to understand ageing as a societal issue (e.g. Government Office for Science 2019), accepting Walker's (2017) call for a social policy for ageing, as the following quotations from two influential reports suggest:

> *Our society are [sic] woefully underprepared. Longer lives can be a great benefit, but there has been a collective failure to address the implications and without urgent action this great boon could turn into a series of miserable crises.* (House of Lords 2013: 1)
> *Ageing populations will create new demands for technologies, products and services, including new care technologies, new housing models and innovative savings products for retirement. We have an obligation to help our older citizens lead independent, fulfilled lives, continuing to contribute to society.* (Department for Business, Energy and Industrial Strategy 2017: 52)

Plate 1.1 Dinner Time at Marylebone Workhouse, 1900.
Source: Alamy

Plate 1.2 Old-age pensions are introduced for the first time in Britain, 1 January
1909

Source: *Chronicle*/Alamy

Each of these quotations contain elements of an optimism associated
with societal obligation and the common good that justifies state interventions, albeit at the local level, as they enable older people to lead more
fulfilling lives throughout the life course. One consequence of these studies

has been the culmination of thinking that recognises ageing as one of the *grand challenges* facing society in the UK (and globally). Interestingly, the political doctrine of the Third Way (Giddens 1998), which entails a neo-liberalist approach to the state and acceptance of the capitalist model of production, advocated a more socially democratic approach to government that impacted public policy on ageing. As a result of the adoption of this approach, market approaches to state social policy were introduced as a new policy direction, offering more citizen choice, but in many cases envisaging a greater role for the third sector in supporting the needs of an ageing population in pursuit of cost-cutting in state provision. Society is arguably returning to some of the Victorian values of voluntarism and charity, as the third sector fills in gaps in state provision (e.g. foodbanks to address poverty). Third-sector interventions are now widely encouraged as a way of developing more community-oriented solutions to some of the problems associated with ageing. This has complemented the extreme resource stretch facing many local authorities and encouraged more partnership working among public sector agencies in grant-bidding activity to support the needs of an ageing society. Social policy on ageing issues has been predominantly focused on two major themes: the cost of maintaining welfare state provision in a future society (i.e. how to fund pensions and healthcare costs) and the cost of social care for an ageing population. In each case, the financial imperative and looming financial crises to which the House of Lords (2013) alluded have been centre stage in most political debates on ageing.

So how has this shifting philosophical position towards understanding ageing as a societal issue contributed to more positive approaches to ageing?

New paradigms on ageing: Active and healthy ageing

More positive approaches to ageing emanate from two specific strands of work that have emerged from United Nations initiatives on active ageing and healthy ageing. Walker (2015) traced the evolution of the active ageing concept to discourses by international governmental organisations like the United Nations' World Health Organization (WHO) in the 1970s, but the idea gathered momentum in the 1980s as developed countries started to recognise the economic costs of ageing. Philosophically, active ageing was shaped by Rowe and Kahn's (1987) model for successful ageing. Walker (2015: 18) outlined the essential principles in Rowe and Kahn's model which were based on (a) a low probability of disease in old age and of disease-related disability; (b) the retention of high levels of cognitive and physical capacity; and (c) active engagement in later life. Despite problems with this concept, its positive outlook on how to enable people in later life stimulated considerable policy debate. An initiative published by the World

Health Organization in 1994 promoted the associated concept of healthy ageing, which it defined as 'the process of developing and maintaining the functional ability that enables wellbeing in older age', and this has been rolled out by bodies such as the European Union and promoted by many governments through the WHO's Decade of Healthy Ageing (2021–2030). Walker (2015: 19–20), in explaining healthy ageing, stated that 'the thinking behind this new approach . . . is expressed perfectly in the WHO dictum "years have been added to life now we must add life to years"', which implied a need to promote more active lifestyles to maintain and enhance the physical and mental health of an ageing population. Both active and healthy ageing as paradigms focus on enhancing the well-being of an ageing population per se, as opposed to simple concerns with social care and institutional care, adopting a more holistic approach to the lives of an ageing population to enhance their well-being. Whether or not these issues are politically or economically motivated in social policy terms, this focus represents a step change in thinking about ageing through enriching well-being.

It is notable that active ageing promotes the adoption of a holistic approach to the lives of the ageing population, in recognition of the factors and barriers that can be addressed to enhance well-being. A central tenet of more active agendas in ageing is to encourage older people to play a more active role in society and take more responsibility for their well-being and happiness, by accessing services and support in a society that is designed for their needs. Globally there are many examples of the implementation of active ageing (e.g. Walker and Aspalter 2015; Zaidi et al. 2018; Boulton-Lewis and Tam 2011; Timonen 2016; Riva et al. 2014; Formosa 2019; Hofäker et al. 2016; Baskaran 2020; Walker 2018). Active ageing has been an underpinning component of how we develop a more practical series of social policies that enable an ageing population to continue to lead the type of life they enjoyed before ageing began to impact their lives. It was in this context that the age-friendly model emerged.

The age-friendly paradigm

Much of the impetus for developing age-friendly programmes has been derived from WHO's Age-Friendly Communities (AFC) model (WHO 2007a) (later broadened to Age-Friendly Cities and Communities), which aimed to improve the physical and social environments that people aged in. The AFC initiative was promoted through the Dublin Declaration on Age-Friendly Cities and Communities in Europe in 2013 where political leaders signed up 60 communities to become age-friendly. By 2020 the WHO Global Network of AFC localities comprised 830 cities and communities in 41 countries. The WHO concept of AFC covers eight domains of human life (e.g. health, long-term care, transport, housing, labour, social protection, information, and communication) that are impacted by different stakeholders (e.g. government, service providers, older people and their families and friends). The WHO objectives that need to be fulfilled for places to become AFC are to combat ageism, to enable older people to achieve more autonomy and to promote WHO's agenda of healthy ageing (Stephens and Breheny 2018). The AFC model hinges upon achieving progress in eight domains (Figure 1.1; with some areas such as the visitor economy notable by their absence), to which we will return in Chapter 2. The AFC model is premised on the walkability of neighbourhoods for residents (Gibney et al. 2020), and is based on Universal Design principles (http://universaldesign. ie), which aim to achieve greater accessibility for all.

The AFC model represents a major rethink on how to approach ageing – it adopts the ethos of co-production rather than just provision of services and environments for ageing people, extending Jones's (2007) debate on the services to support healthy ageing that are needed to encourage independent living among an ageing population. Philosophically, this is also part of a rebirth of thinking on civil rights that stems from the 1960s, stimulated by a re-evaluation of the civil-society concept whereby people are not excluded from participating in society by barriers, and reiterating the importance of liberal concepts of social obligation and the common good. Numerous theoretical agendas from the same period (e.g. the 'right to the city', initially

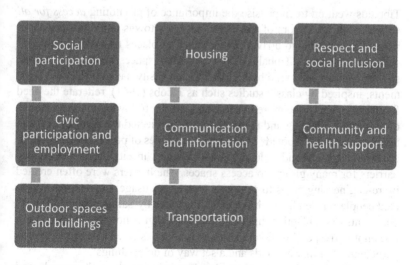

Figure 1.1 Elements of an age-friendly city, according to the age-friendly communities domains set out by the WHO

advocated and developed by Lefebvre (1968) and Rawls (1971)) significantly contributed toward explaining why a people-centred agenda was so
important in areas such as ageing. Such studies present a powerful narrative
around the unequivocal argument that urban policy should focus on how it
affects the less fortunate. These issues were developed in Lefebvre's later
work (Lefebvre 1976, 1991), in which issues of justice and space were conditioned by politics, place and the policies that are developed and implemented for cities and other locations. The main argument that Lefebvre is
making is that space is not an empty void. Instead, it is 'filled with politics,
ideology, and other forces shaping our lives' (Soja 2010: 19). Therefore,
social policy has a key role to play in recognising the rights of specific
groups like the older population, so they can reclaim the city and spaces
where barriers exist. One good example is reflected in architecture and
planning. Tibbalds (2001: 14) reinforced these views, arguing that 'public
places within a town belong to the people of that town' and developing the
concept of the public realm, which comprises:

> *those places that make up the public realm come in many shapes, and*
> *sizes and uses. They include streets, squares, public footpaths, parks,*
> *and open spaces and extend, also, to riversides and seafronts. These*
> *places all belong to the wider community. It is so important never to*
> *forget that they are there for their use, benefit and enjoyment.* (Tibbalds*
> 2001: 13)

Tibbalds went on to emphasise the importance of promoting *access for all*
activities for all sectors of the community, as 'towns and cities are about
human contact and so arrival points, meeting places or places to congre-
gate are important' (Tibbalds 2001: 57). Such spaces need to be legible,
so they can be easily read by their users, and easily navigable. These arguments, inspired by classic studies such as Jacobs (1961), reiterate the need
for urban spaces to be more liveable and usable, following almost 50 years
of modernist planning and architecture that neglected the realities of using
urban space daily. Tibbalds (2001) cited examples of poorly designed modernist architecture and redevelopment schemes in cities that had created
barriers for many groups to access spaces. The barriers were often created
by re-engineering cities to prioritise greater car usage, but as a result created people-unfriendly environments, illustrated by Salingaros' (2021: n.p.)
comments that 'adaptive, human-centered design is not popular because it
does not correspond to favored design typologies . . . Professional inertia
perpetuates familiar methods and a set way of doing things'.

Other theoretical perspectives that have shaped the AFC agenda and
thinking include environmental gerontology, which Schwarz and Scheidt

(2013: 1) define as seeking to understand the 'continually changing interrelations between aging people and their sociophysical environment and how these relationships shape the human aging progression'; which, in practical terms, means that 'through involvement in modification and the design of housing and public places, practitioners in the field strive for enhancing the well-being of older adults as they age'. Wahl and Weisman (2003) outlined the development of environmental gerontology from the 1940s onwards, highlighting the contribution of environmental psychology and social gerontology in the 1950s, fields that focused on the environment's impact on human development. 'Other contextual influences included the Chicago school of urban sociology in the twenties (e.g. Park, Burgess and McKenzie 1925), the writings of Lewin in the thirties and forties (e.g. Lewin 1935), and the emergence of environmental psychology in the sixties and seventies' (Wahl and Weisman 2003: 617–618), all of which focused on 'people' in the urban environment. Kelley et al. (2019) pointed to the tendency in environmental gerontology to over-focus on micro-spatial issues, such as the family, home and experience of places, to the detriment of macro-environmental issues, such as policy and the political economy of ageing. This was described as *microfication*, a preoccupation with the immediacy of everyday life and the barriers facing the ageing population. The unintended consequence of such an approach was that *erasure* occurred (i.e. the elderly population became unseen in policy terms). Extrapolating that into AFC research, Kelley et al. (2019) argued for a more critical sociological perspective that does not simply focus on individualism and micro-level factors associated with ageism, as these are often determined by macro-environmental factors that sometimes lead to the exclusion of ageing people in urban renewal schemes.

The WHO advocates an evidence-based approach to communities seeking to become AFC, based on consulting residents to create AFC environments and then sharing the outcomes with their AFC network.[1] To be truly inclusive, this process needs to be broadened to include the diverse range of users of these environments, including visitors, who are not included in the WHO model. The AFC model has been successfully implemented in some countries, where the state has promoted this agenda (e.g. Ireland and Canada; see Plouffe and Kalache 2011) as a new holistic approach to ageing. The sources on AFC development are dominated by grey literature linked with the reports and projects commissioned by many public bodies to advise them on becoming AFC. Understanding the AFC movement and the ideology behind it also helps to illustrate how a shift has occurred in thinking whereby ageing people are now asked to participate in and influence the creation of the age-friendly environments and services they need to facilitate independent living.

The emergent academic literature on AFC initiatives is characterised by several weaknesses in the way the knowledge is compiled, constructed and disseminated, which illustrates the need for an in-depth study of one country. First, the majority of published academic studies reiterate in considerable detail how and why the WHO AFC initiative developed, creating a highly repetitive body of knowledge. Second, theorisation remains weakly articulated in many of the studies, with few examples of critical reflective analysis from practitioners. Third, the grey literature is largely based on manuals and 'how to' guidance for communities. Fourth, the research literature is inherently biased in terms of the perspectives offered, invariably characterising AFC as an unequivocally positive step forward (even where these steps have faltered due to resourcing). Criticism is sometimes muted or diluted, which is somewhat surprising given the principles of academic research, whereby both the strengths and weaknesses of AFC social policy and practice should be balanced so that they contribute to knowledge and practice. Fifth, there is a lack of reflexivity and a reluctance to draw parallels with other attempts in society to address 'isms' such as racism, sexism and disablism to understand how this may help address ageism (Sun Life 2020) as an ingrained aspect of many developed societies. Sixth, there are very few empirically informed analyses of different countries to permit a comparative analysis of the AFC paradigm. Instead, many papers are case studies of provinces, areas or cities and so comparisons cannot easily be drawn and nor can wider conclusions be derived from progress in wider society with the AFC paradigm. Accordingly, this opportunity to explore in-depth a countrywide study of age-friendly implementation is timely and important in terms of advancing knowledge and understanding of issues at a macro level – in this case, in the UK.

Why a book on age-friendly practices in the UK?

This short book provides a focused but comprehensive assessment of AFC initiatives in the UK based on in-depth interviews with the AFC leads in each locality, in order to understand what being an AFC community means in practice, how the schemes have developed and evolved, and what outcomes have been achieved. It is the first national systematic study of age-friendly practices in the UK, examining their development and operation; other studies have been in-depth analyses or overviews, or case studies of specific countries, meaning this will be a benchmark study for other countries. Given that it is based on in-depth interviews with the people who are intimately involved with the construction and implementation of social policy at a community level, the book potentially has a global significance as there is growing interest in how countries have approached AFCs, and what can be learned from people intimately involved in the programmes of work. Therefore, as an exemplar of the age-friendly movement in practice, this book provides an evidence base that can easily be transferred to other countries to measure progress in becoming age-friendly grounded in practitioner experiences. Whilst a vast literature is emerging from an interdisciplinary perspective, much of the discussion is based on academic commentary as opposed to the voices of those people involved in developing and implementing AFC practices. This study is unique at a national scale because it develops new evidence from primary data as opposed to relying solely on secondary data and documentary analysis. We hope this will be both a novel and concise review of the age-friendly movement in the UK that will stimulate further discussion, debate and research on this popular theme.

To structure the study, a series of research questions were developed from the existing literature on AFCs to provide a deeper understanding of the following issues:

1 How and why have age-friendly initiatives developed in the UK? This encompasses the factors that have motivated their development, alongside the championing of these initiatives in public and third-sector organisations and the political importance of this area of policy and practice.

2 Who implements age-friendly programmes and what challenges do they face? Here, we seek to provide a human context to the study by understanding the people that champion and facilitate these schemes. Specifically, what types of work do they undertake, what are their backgrounds and how do they view ageing?

3 What are the key features of the age-friendly programmes in operation? What types of activities and projects have they undertaken? What types of partnership working exist, and how do they broaden engagement with other stakeholders such as businesses?

To address these questions, this book reports the findings of the first national study of the age-friendly movement in the UK. Data collection was completed in 2021 based on in-depth interviews with the majority of the age-friendly leads who participated in our research.

Structure of the book

Chapter 2 critically reviews how and why the age-friendly movement has been embraced and where this has occurred globally, as well as its scope, using several examples of countries that have implemented this social policy framework. The chapter also introduces the type of community development model that AFC development has adopted. In Chapter 3, in-depth discussion of the empirical research commences, drawing upon the existing literature and in-depth interviews, which provide a rich tapestry of views and assessments of issues from age-friendly officers or senior managers who oversee the age-friendly schemes in their localities. The chapter will offer insights into the nature of the people managing these schemes, their divergent career backgrounds and expertise and their perception of ageing as a societal issue. The research findings explore why certain localities have chosen specific age-friendly pathways and how these are often conditioned or shaped by national or local political agendas. Chapter 4 continues the primary research analysis by focusing on how age-friendly schemes are evaluated as a model of community development. The key role of network development and stakeholder engagement is discussed as a means by which wider development opportunities have been progressed and how funding opportunities and grant aid have helped some schemes to make major inroads towards making their communities age-friendly. The scope for the greater integration of business perspectives is also examined, along with the embryonic nature of the visitor economy as an area for growth and development. The final chapter reviews the implications of the study. It provides a critique of the age-friendly model, highlighting some of its challenges and weaknesses, as well as looking at how it might interconnect with other agendas such as sustainability.

Note

1 'The WHO Age-Friendly Cities Framework', World Health Organization: https://extranet.who.int/agefriendlyworld/age-friendly-cities-framework/#:~:text=The%20WHO%20Age-friendly%20Cities%20framework%20developed%20in%20the%20Global,and%20interact%2

2 Understanding the nature of the age-friendly movement

Introduction

The emergence of the age-friendly movement has developed alongside numerous theoretical developments in gerontology and the burgeoning literature on ageing within the social sciences. As a paradigm, it has stimulated a great deal of new thinking spanning both policy settings and academia, with many practitioners endorsing its significance through creating Age-Friendly Community (AFC) programmes globally. As a positive response to ingrained levels of ageism in society, it has acted as a counterbalance to the 'invisibility' of older people (Swift and Steeden 2020) in many of the new agendas in society such as equal opportunities, and in the context of a raft of 'isms', such as racism, disablism and gender equality, all of which apply to ageing people as well. Butler (2006: 11) suggests that ageism is 'a process of systematic stereotyping and discrimination against people because they are old . . . it is deeply ingrained in society, categorising old people as senile, rigid in thought and manner, and old fashioned in morality and skills' (Butler 2006: 41). The age-friendly paradigm seeks to reverse this negative discriminatory behaviour with actions to redress issues of social injustice around simple issues such as improving accessibility. Age-friendly has a more compassionate tone than terminology such as old or aged, which evokes negative imagery, with a more enabling narrative that does not view age as a problem. Instead, it views older age as a stage in life that society needs to accommodate in the same way it has normalised our approach to many 'isms' under a equality banner, to build a more inclusive community and to challenge injustice and prejudice. From a political perspective, the age-friendly concept provides older people with a voice and redresses their invisibility.

People and their needs are at the heart of the age-friendly agenda. A careful reading of many of the narratives opposing the continued industrialisation and urbanisation of the world in the 1960s and 1970s shows that they display elements of the age-friendly movement, highlighting the

DOI: 10.4324/9781003319801-2

needs of people who are being omitted from a growth agenda. Whitaker and Browne's (1971) *Parks for People* reinforced these arguments, observing the population *longevity* crisis facing many countries and the necessity of the availability of parks and open space at a neighbourhood level. These spaces were viewed as necessary to offset the dehumanising effects of continued infrastructure provision for cars and of high-rise developments that were transforming many urban environments in the twentieth century. Urban growth and development were negating the human connection with a sense of place at a local level, as urban environments became less people-friendly, isolating them as they progressed through the latter stages of life. The isolation was felt physically, socially and emotionally, as grand regeneration schemes embodied the planning profession's dominant idiom of 'planning for' rather than 'planning with' people.

Almost 30 years after Whitaker and Browne's (1971) visionary arguments for parks for people as a place of refuge from the dehumanising effects of rapid urbanisation, Tibbalds (2001) highlighted failures to plan the urban environment with people's changing needs in mind. The transition from people-friendly to age-friendly was a natural corollary in this broad advocacy of people as more than passive users of cities. Even recent studies, such as Sennett (2018), continue to argue for people-friendly cities. The simple, indisputable argument is that better planned and designed places enhance the physical and social fabric of those places. In this way, the urban environment has a more positive impact on the health and wellbeing of the population (Marmot et al. 2010). At the heart of the arguments on enhancing the urban fabric is the need to encourage people to engage in physical exercise by living active lives. Their choice or ability to do this is governed by a multiplicity of factors such as pollution, access to green and open space, transport and housing. Such factors also condition the level of community participation and perceived levels of social isolation among the ageing population. Greater participation in physical exercise helps people live well with age-related conditions such as dementia and benefit from increased levels of social participation as well as leading to general reductions in levels of stress and depression. Consequently, policy interventions to create better living environments for an ageing population are critical if they will help people live longer at home with dignity and independence and reduce state social care and health costs. Key arguments around accessibility suggest that initiatives such as AFCs lead to broader enhancements in this area, and so offer improved access for a wider range of people of all ages. This unintended consequence is a beneficial outcome for the common good. The significance of the age-friendly movement and its ability to shift thinking around how to approach ageing more inclusively is expressed succinctly in the strategy on ageing for Wales:

- Our vision is an age friendly Wales that supports people of all ages to live and age well.
- We want to create a Wales where everyone looks forward to growing older.
- A Wales where individuals can take responsibility for their own health and well-being whilst feeling confident that support will be available and easily accessible if needed.
- A Wales where ageism does not limit potential or affect the quality of services older people receive.
- Ultimately, we want to be a nation that celebrates age and, in line with the UN Principles for Older Persons, a nation that upholds the independence, participation, care, self-fulfilment and dignity of older people at all times.

(Welsh Government 2021: 9)

So what does becoming an AFC mean and what are the key principles and practices that have to be put in place to implement it?

The scope of the age-friendly agenda: The World Health Organization model

Rémillard-Boilard (2019) traced the roots of the AFC model to 1982 and a United Nations conference that was followed by the development of active-ageing policies (see the timeline and key milestones at https://extranet.who.int/agefriendlyworld/age-friendly-cities-framework/). The World Health Organization (WHO 2002) defined an age-friendly city as being capable of engaging with the active-ageing agenda as a 'process of optimising opportunities for health, participation and security in order to enhance quality of life as people age' (WHO 2002: 12). In 2005, the age-friendly programme was introduced at the International Association of Gerontology and Geriatrics World Congress and in the following year, it was formally launched through the WHO Age-Friendly Cities project, with the framework set out in two documents (WHO 2007a,b). The main purpose of the age-friendly city programme as it was originally conceived was to understand the needs of an ageing population, with focus groups a key element in understanding community design needs in order 'to improve their physical and social environments [and for these] to become better places in which to grow old'. From the initial scoping work associated with the programme, eight domains that influence the quality of life of older people were identified, as shown in Figure 1.1. Each domain had a checklist of different criteria associated with age-friendliness (WHO 2007a,b); the checklist was critiqued, and the criteria used by Plouffe et al. (2016). In 2010, the World Health Organization (WHO) also established a website titled Global Network of Age-Friendly Cities and Communities (https://extranet.who.int/agefriend lyworld/who-network/), recognising the wider application of the concept beyond an urban setting. The network consists of 333 cities and communities in 47 countries, comprising over 298 million people worldwide, and is constantly expanding.

The WHO has previously outlined its mission and ideology on becoming age-friendly, arguing as follows:

> *Creating environments that are truly age-friendly requires action in many sectors: health, long-term care, transport, housing, labour, social protection, information and communication, and by many actors – government, service providers, civil society, older people and their organizations, families and friends. It also requires action at multiple levels of government.*

Figure 2.1 outlines the dual role of the WHO and stakeholders in seeking to create age-friendly environments. The WHO argues that

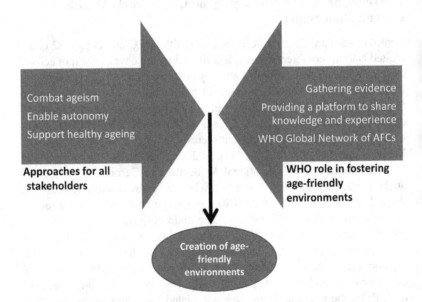

Figure 2.1 WHO vision of how its collaborating partners contribute to creating age-friendly environments

Source: Developed from https://extranet.who.int/agefriendlyworld/age-friendly-practices/

in practical terms, age-friendly environments are free from physical and social barriers and supported by policies, systems, services, products and technologies that:

* *promote health and build and maintain physical and mental capacity across the life course; and*
* *enable people, even when experiencing capacity loss, to continue to do the things they value.*

(https://extranet.who.int/agefriendlyworld/
age-friendly-practices/).

As Figure 2.2 shows, age-friendly practices have a twofold impact in enhancing older people's abilities and their needs.

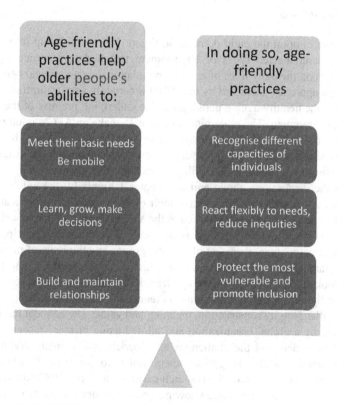

Figure 2.2 The WHO's summary of what age-friendly practices contribute to older people's lives

Source: Developed from https://extranet.who.int/agefriendlyworld/age-friendly-practices/

Figures 2.1 and 2.2 show that the WHO standard is useful in setting out broad objectives; but what does the term age-friendly mean, and what are the different interpretations of that term?

Age-friendly: A nebulous concept?

The term age-friendly is far from a straightforward concept to understand and deconstruct. Most studies point to the World Health Organization (WHO 2007a: 1) definition that states:

> *Age-friendly environments aim to encourage active and healthy living by optimizing health, stimulating inclusion and enabling well-being in older age. They adapt physical environments, social environments and municipal services to the needs of older people with varying capacities.*

This hinges upon the eight domains in Figure 1.1, which group into these three interconnected types of environment that underpin, structure and impact upon the daily lives of an older population. From a critical perspective, the approach promoted by the WHO is certainly very aspirational and stresses the healthy-ageing paradigm as the underlying premise of the age-friendly argument. The underpinning aim is to make an AFC a good place to grow old, and in which to remain independent for as long as possible. But critics of the healthy-ageing paradigm criticise this approach for its targeting of those who are able and willing to embrace that agenda.

As the discussions above and in Chapter 1 highlight, the antecedents of the age-friendly movement have their roots in many philosophical and political agendas that can be traced to the Victorian era and that resurfaced in the 1960s and 1970s around issues such as community participation, discrimination, empowerment of specific groups and the issue of poor service planning by public bodies. These historical perspectives tend to be overlooked in the debates on the age-friendly model, with most researchers implicitly accepting the paradigm, its tenets and the broad concept without challenging its construction, meaning and value. The concept has been devised by a global organization and piloted using primary research that seeks to understand the challenges and barriers facing many communities in dealing with ageing as a societal issue. To the cynic, it is perhaps a natural development of the research carried out in the 1980s on service quality, service provision and knowing your customers' needs from a public policy perspective. This was a paradigm that developed in the neoliberalist state in the 1980s, as privatisation and cuts to state provision of services to communities took place in a reaction to the spiralling costs of services. Similarly, the theoretical debates being raised on new municipalism, explored later, connect with the age-friendly arguments about community development meeting local needs as a pragmatic solution to the decline in state resources to support ageing.

Yet these ideals do not adequately engage with some of the deeper philosophical debates that emerge around the age-friendly model – such as what it means to the people it is targeting, and how it sits alongside the challenge of defining, understanding and encapsulating ageing as a concept. 'Age-friendly' is also a state of mind and way of thinking that seeks to treat people in a fair and impartial manner. The age-friendly concept at a macro level would appear to have meaning to policy-makers and practitioners, at whose level adaptations, changes and specific needs can be articulated. For the individual, the meaning of age-friendly is a broad and perhaps ambiguous term, especially as existing research suggests (see Blakie 1999) that the way in which 'older age' is constructed and understood by individuals needs to be more flexible and fluid rather than classifying people according to calendar age. For the purposes of what is meant by age-friendly, this is very much in the eye of the beholder, because no two people are the same. Furthermore, the capabilities of individuals vary considerably in terms of accessibility needs. Given there are no service standards for being classified as age-friendly, this also leaves the interpretation of what is age-friendly from a supply (service provider) and demand (the user) perspective open to misinterpretation. In service quality research, this is defined as a gap between customer expectations and the actual service provision (Parasuraman et al. 1985). The age-friendly narrative leaves open the potential for the perceived degree of age-friendliness to be exaggerated by users/consumers, and to make it hard to make an assessment of whether a service or location really is as age-friendly as the label suggests. The Parasuraman et al. (1985) model that stimulated a whole generation of service quality research does highlight several key considerations that users of age-friendly services may well use in forming an opinion on age-friendliness including reliability, responsiveness, competence to perform the service, accessibility/approachability, courtesy, credibility, security and knowing the customer. Other more tangible elements that may be evaluated as part of age-friendliness include the physical facilities that are being accessed and used. With these issues in mind, what does it mean for a community when it decides to become age-friendly?

Becoming an age-friendly community

The criteria for becoming age-friendly are set out in the WHO age-friendly communities process – the Age-Friendly Cycle (i.e. sending a commitment letter to the WHO Age-Friendly Network to register the community's intent; creating a baseline assessment of age-friendly infrastructure needs; devising a strategy and action plan; implementation; and evaluation). Buffel et al. (2019) explained the five-year commitment to the WHO age-friendly membership scheme This is illustrated in Figure 2.3, based on Buffel et al.'s (2019) illustration of the time frames involved in the cycle, to clarify how the eight domains are dealt with as part of a systematic process to make a community age-friendly. In the example presented by Buffel et al. (2019: 31), an interconnected four-step process needed to be followed in order to gain membership, which involved: (1) planning (2) implementation (3) evaluation and (4) improvement. In practice this meant

> *in the planning stage: the establishment of mechanisms to involve older people in all stages of the age-friendly cities process; a comprehensive baseline assessment of the age-friendliness of the city; development of a three year citywide action plan based on assessment of findings; and identification of indicators to monitor progress against this plan.*
> (Buffel et al. 2019: 31)

The application of these principles in developing an AFC is illustrated in two examples in Table 2.1, which outline how Manchester and Brussels implemented the process. As Table 2.1 shows, there is considerable flexibility in the way individual communities approach the age-friendly criteria and assess the best way forward for their locality in terms of each domain and the resulting policies and actions adopted. Buffel et al. (2019), examining the comparative experience of Manchester and Brussels, demonstrate the similarity in the conceptual frameworks and organisational

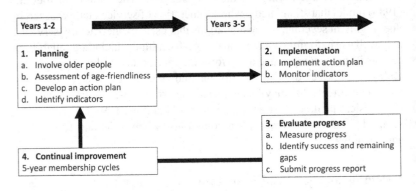

Figure 2.3 The WHO age-friendly process

Source: After Buffel et al. (2019)

Table 2.1 Frameworks of age-friendly approaches by the WHO: Brussels and Manchester

WHO*	Brussels**	Manchester***
Outdoor spaces and buildings	**Community safety** • Organising information sessions about crime prevention • Increasing feelings of safety through the presence of city guards (i.e., prevention agents) • Promoting cooperation between the police, the city council, court justice, and local associations • Coordinated police actions in response to missing older people (c.f., project 'senior focus')	**Lifetime neighbourhoods** • Working toward accessible and well-designed living environments in which residents are not excluded by age • Working toward becoming an environmentally Green City, with older people as important partners in achieving this Community safety • Preventing doorstep crime • Expanding initiatives to reduce crime and anti-social behaviour on and around public transport
Housing	**Housing** • Ensuring that ordinary homes are suitable for older people • Promoting home adaptations and modifications • Supporting alternative housing options (e.g., group living schemes, intergenerational house-sharing)	**Housing** • Ensuring that ordinary homes are suitable for older people • Promoting Design for Access standards • Delivering additional new homes and affordable housing delivering new-care units
Transportation	**Mobility** • Making community transport more accessible and flexible including demand-responsive services • Ensuring a senior lens in urban mobility plans • Supporting traffic-calming initiatives • Promoting existing car-sharing and bike-sharing initiatives • Improving the 'walkability' of the city	**Transport** • Making community transport more accessible and flexible including demand-responsive services • Improving general bus services with better driving and more shelters with seats • 'Bikeability' training for older workers • Improving road safety and pavements

(Continued)

Table 2.1 (Continued)

WHO*	Brussels**	Manchester***
Social participation	**Social life** • Improving information about activities and events • Offering a wide variety of activities (e.g., in local pavilions/meeting places for older people) • Promoting older people's participation in projects and actions concerning public life in the city (e.g., in district forums) • Supporting initiatives aimed at combating social isolation • Actively recruiting older volunteers • Organising an annual 'seniors' week' with various activities	**Cross-cutting themes: Improving engagement; improving relationships** • Extending opportunities for older people's involvement in decision making, project delivery, and service design • Expanding alliances of front-line staff, community groups, and older people • Extending opportunities for volunteering • Completing connected Generations Together programmes and evaluating their impact • Reviewing best practice for a guide to tackle loneliness
Respect and social inclusion	• Actively involving the senior advisory board in all age-friendly projects and policies	**Cross-cutting theme: Promoting equality**
Civic participation and employment	**Socio-economic situation** • Combating poverty through coordinated provision of social housing for older people • Promoting volunteering and engagement in associations • Recognising the wide range of capacities and resources among older people	Income and employment • Support over-50s to stay in work • Support over-50s in steps towards the world of work (especially men who are made redundant and people on benefits due to mental health problems) • Promote and support volunteering and learning opportunities for over-50s

Communication and information

Information
- Centralising information regarding services, activities and organisations for older people in a 'senior guide'
- Providing a bi-monthly magazine offering an overview of leisure activities for older people
- Facilitating information access (information sessions in senior centres and 'pavilions'; internet courses in libraries; easy access to/discount purchases and rents of computers)

Culture and learning
- Promoting more accessible and better marketed activities
- Supporting community-based and intergenerational learning activities
- Reaching minority-ethnic elders and those in disadvantaged areas

Community support and health services

Health
- Improving information about access to available services
- Better coordination of the fragmented supply of home-care services

Healthy aging
Care and support services
- Developing intermediate care best practice
- Introducing more integrated teams and multifactorial assessment
- Improving home care and developing more comprehensive, flexible, and culturally sensitive services
- Removing barriers to minority-ethnic elders

Note. *For a more detailed description of the WHO framework and domains, see the document *Global Age-Friendly Cities: A Guide* (WHO 2007a).
**The analysis for the Brussels age-friendly city framework is based on internal documents that have been developed by the City Council on the basis of the research findings of the Belgian Ageing Studies project in order to be admitted into the WHO Global Network of Age-Friendly Cities and Communities.
***The analysis for the Manchester age-friendly city framework is based on the Manchester Ageing Strategy as developed in the policy document *Manchester: A Great Place to Grow Older 2010–2020* (see McGarry & Morris 2011).
Source: Buffel et al. (2019: 32–4) reproduced with permission from Routledge.

models they developed to implement an age-friendly programme. Differences emerged in the emphasis within the social policy focus in each locality: Brussels used social housing as a tool to help tackle poverty, whilst in contrast, there was a greater focus on ethnic diversity in Manchester. In Brussels, the development of AFC outdoor spaces and buildings prioritised community safety and crime prevention. Manchester, however, identified the initial use of lifetime neighbourhoods and then age-friendly neighbourhoods after 2012, underlining the significance of a community development model.

This short discussion of the comparative experience of two of the earliest cities to join the WHO programme suggests that

> *Manchester has a stronger tradition . . . in developing age-friendly policies. This is especially the case in relation to Manchester's culturally sensitive and targeted approaches toward minority ethnic elders and those in deprived urban areas; the city's development of 'lifetime and age-friendly neighbourhoods', including the integration of age-friendly principles into the regeneration and design in urban spaces; and the way in which Manchester is able to brand and promote the age-friendly approach.* (Buffel et al. 2019: 42–3)

Based on the experiences of Manchester and Brussels, Buffel et al. (2019) identified a range of success factors in becoming age-friendly that include:

- The integration of policies for older people into the wider management of the city, including its urban redevelopment. Here the success lies in addressing many of the criticisms of the current urban form and structure of cities and communities, so that the natural cycle of urban redevelopment pays attention to ageing issues. Buffel et al. (2019) describe this as mainstreaming ageing issues, whereby it is critical to cross-cut local government policies and procedures to make ageing a core issue in redevelopment plans rather than a supplementary consideration.
- Ensuring that the mainstreaming embeds all areas of city activity in terms of both social and public policy reflecting community stakeholders' needs and views, so that planning takes place with a broad, all-encompassing agenda rather than a top-down approach, in order to make it more inclusive.

From a theoretical perspective, the framing of the age-friendly paradigm may be interpreted using the new municipalism framework (Thompson 2021) with its focus on challenging the neoliberalist policies of the 1980s and 1990s. The result is a shift towards more interventionist policies focused on greater levels of social innovation to address societal problems at the local level. In the case of ageing, this involves greater collaboration between the third sector and business with a common purpose of focusing on the everyday experiences of people to enhance their well-being. Such collaboration helps to fill a void where austerity and state centrism has left grand societal challenges like ageing as a major challenge for local areas. Institutional change, as described in the case of Manchester embedding a theme such as ageing as a key policy focus, displays distinct strands of new municipalism. The fundamental shift in thinking is in engaging people to help co-produce a space that is appropriate to a wider range of needs, with a strategy-led and more democratic approach to planning to improve well-being. This is in sharp contrast to the legacy of former neoliberalist policies, which were essentially place-based, designed to target societal problems, rather than taking a more holistic and embedded approach. Buffel et al. (2019) situate the age-friendly narrative in a similar context whereby the development of age-friendly policies engages a wide range of stakeholders to foster a collaborative and cooperative approach. But above all, the age-friendly approach embraces a senior lens. As Menec et al. (2011) argue, that lens is important in enabling an ageing population to identify issues and priorities for action. With this in mind, it is pertinent to briefly review some of the key themes in the emergent literature on age-friendly issues so as to understand the developing knowledge base and the central agendas for research and practice, as a prelude to moving on to the principal focus of the research questions set out in Chapter 1.

The existing research literature on age-friendly issues: A selective overview

The extant research literature on age-friendly initiatives at a global scale indicates that the work can be classified into four specific groups: books designed to popularise the theme, or monographs that compile a range of current thinking on a specific topic, or which adopt a generic approach; review articles that offer commentary on the current state of thinking on AFCs or one aspect of age-friendly work; a substantial grey literature on various facets of the age-friendly journey of localities; how-to guides and some studies offering a degree of foresight; and an expansive range of scientific journal articles, examining specific themes as well as reflective pieces, typically book chapters from academics and practitioners. In terms of books, some of the most notable examples include Samuel (2021), Beard (2022) and Scharlach and Lehning (2016), all of which focus on specific countries and cities.

The first comparative study based on an edited collection of papers (i.e. Moulaert and Garon 2015) highlighted the importance of drawing cross-city and -country comparisons in order to understand the similarities, differences and developments in age-friendly practices. The same theme was exemplified in the Buffel et al. (2019) analysis of Manchester and Brussels discussed earlier. More thematic analyses are evident in the studies by Stafford (2019), Buffel, Handler and Phillipson (2018), Chao (2018) and Caro and Fitzgerald (2018), alongside associated books on ageing such as Stroud and Walker (2012). Within these books, the individual chapters provide a series of snapshots of countries, framed as case studies of how age-friendly schemes have been established and developed. Yet synthesis of progress towards becoming age-friendly in individual countries remains partial and limited and must be assembled in many cases from the broader grey and academic literature. There is a clear research gap in the existing knowledge to systematically evaluate the experiences of age-friendly schemes within entire countries in order to understand the multifaceted nature of their practices and implementation.

A number of review articles which seek to offer broad assessments of progress in the field exist within journals. One of the early overviews in the field, by Plouffe and Kalache (2011), outlined much of the familiar narrative on how the WHO initiative emerged and covers similar ground to the subsequent review by Rémillard-Boilard (2019). Most journal articles tend to provide this evolutionary review as contextual background. Scharlach's (2012) study focused on the development of age-friendly initiatives in the United States. Other studies such as Buffel et al. (2012) outlined the potential of AFCs from a critical social policy perspective in relation to the age-friendly paradigm along with the inherent contradictions and issues associated with the age-friendly approach. Buffel and Phillipson (2016) examined AFCs from the perspective of peoples' rights, drawing upon Soja (2013) and Harvey's (2003) work on spatial justice which we discussed in Chapter 1. Fitzgerald and Caro's (2014) preamble to a special issue of the *Journal of Aging and Social Policy* provided an overview of the WHO initiative but also introduced the significance of factors not discussed as part of the WHO criteria, such as the influence of climate and weather and topography, which make each place's AFC journey unique. The degree of social and civic organisation, and social and political organisations (formal and informal) were a key determinant of the success of designing and implementing AFCs, a feature examined by Joy's (2018) review of policy issues in Toronto. Biggs and Carr (2015) found that the problems with developing AFCs were identified in three domains: political and administrative incapacity to manage such cross-cutting programmes; cost-cutting by the public sector; and the design of the programmes developed as part of the AFC scheme.

Xiang et al. (2021) examined 231 publications associated with AFCs and identified three broad themes: (1) the characteristics of AFCs as specific communities, reflecting the particular features of each city or community, which are far more wide-ranging than its demographic structure; (2) the way WHO criteria had been applied to specific AFCs (as illustrated in Table 2.1); and (3) the measurement of age-friendliness of cities and communities. To date, much of the research literature has been published in a wide range of ageing journals (and a number of localities-focused journals such as *Cities*). Consequently, the wider dissemination to reach a broader social science audience has been a slow process, aside from the books aimed at a general audience. Much of the initial focus in age-friendly research, as Xiang et al. (2021) demonstrated, was on health, social protection, information and communications, housing, urban development, transport, education, long-term care and employment. In somewhat surprising findings, Xiang et al. (2021) illustrated that age-friendly business was a secondary issue. This is a significant oversight in the WHO criteria, as business is one of the major areas that ageing people interact with on a daily basis in much the same way that they interact with the three broad domains, the physical environment, social environment and municipal services. Given the nature of the consumer society we live in, interactions with businesses are a daily occurrence, especially in the service provision for older people outside of municipal delivery, in the daily touchpoints with business.

Rémillard-Boilard (2018) provided an in-depth analysis of the way the age-friendly initiative had developed in the UK, highlighting the coordination and support provided by the Centre for Ageing Better. Similar reviews of Canada and Ireland exist, which we discuss on p. 45. These are complemented by the numerous case studies in Fitzgerald and Caro (2018) and Buffel et al. (2019) that cover familiar material on AFCs. As Buffel and Phillipson's (2018: 179–180) critique of the age-friendly movement suggested, that movement is about 'challenging social inequality, widening participation, coproducing age-friendly communities, codesigning age-friendly environments, encouraging multisectorial and multidisciplinary collaboration [and] integrating research with policy'. In their manifesto for age-friendly development, Buffel, Handler and Phillipson (2018) suggested it hinged upon engaging with a new urban agenda from a more holistic perspective. Yet one could argue that even these agendas are too narrow, when acknowledging that 44.7% of the world's population live in rural areas. In the UK, for example, 9.7 million people live in rural areas (17.1% of the overall population) and 82.9% in urban areas (DEFRA 2021). But within the urban category, there are also very significant differences. For example, 5.3 million people in England and Wales live in coastal areas which are technically classified as towns, and where small populations are located over a dispersed area they are classified as rural settlements). But coastal communities have very different attributes to non-coastal towns, not least because of their accessibility and the seasonal activities associated with the visitor economy in those areas. In other words, as Table 2.2 suggests, a more nuanced approach to place is needed in relation to age-friendliness, because many coastal areas have a higher concentration of elderly residents

Table 2.2 Agendas for age-friendly research: Specific issues and challenges

New urban agendas (after Buffel and Phillipson 2018)	Rural areas	Coastal areas
Smart cities	Complexity of rural experiences, ranging from near urban to remoter rural areas	Poverty and deprivation associated with seasonal employment and seasonal services
Healthy cities	Small communities and limited service provision	Poor housing
Sustainable cities	Diversity of experiences	Over-concentration of elderly in some coastal areas exacerbated by in-migration and over-concentration of rates of dementia
Inclusive cities	Reliance upon rural networks/neighbours/relatives due to poor transport access	Social exclusion
Innovation and governance	High costs of travel	Vulnerable groups clustered near the coast, where many care homes are located
Climate change	Asset gaps	
Employment creation	Limited funding	
Partnership working	Human potential and capacity for volunteering and partnership working is limited	
	Limited access to the sources of urban power; marginalised people	
	Complex governance models where rural areas' services and management span different spatial levels of government	

Source: Buffel and Phillipson (2018); the authors

than other regions. These locales also have a greater proportion of ageing people living with conditions such as dementia, as the Alzheimer's
Society interactive map of clusters of dementia in the UK shows (www.
dementiastatistics.org/statistics/dementia-maps/). For example, the largest
cluster is on the south coast in the Christchurch Parliamentary Constitu-
ency, where 2.8% of the population have dementia diagnoses. The largest
absolute numbers of people with dementia are in the North, East and West
Devon Clinical Commissioning Group health district, where almost 15,500
have a dementia diagnosis. In the case of rural areas, for example, these
face specific difficulties in becoming age-friendly, with a smaller pool of
people to assist in their journey along with acute difficulties in data collection (see Russell et al. 2021). The neglect of rural areas in AFCs was
also reiterated by Sánchez-González et al. (2020). McCrillis et al.'s (2021)
analysis of rural Ontario confirmed many of these findings, also noting
that one size does not fit all in the AFC model, and pointing to the significant challenges faced by rural areas with regard to long-term financial
sustainability, which impacts the implementation process. As Menec et al.
(2021) found in a study of age-friendly schemes in Manitoba, Canada, an
area characterised by its remote rural attributes, six types of AFCs existed:
those which were active; those in hiatus; those which had been reorganised;
those which had stalled; those which had been discontinued; and those that
had never got off the ground, all of which reinforces the arguments on the
unique challenges facing rural areas.

Rémillard-Boilard et al.'s (2021) review used a case-study approach to
explore the issues that age-friendly programmes faced, identifying four priorities for further development: addressing the public perception of older age;
bringing key actors into age-friendly actions; meeting the very diverse needs
of the older demographic; and making enhancements to the delivery of age-
friendly programmes. Torku et al. (2021) reiterated some of these themes, but
their systematic review of 98 publications on AFC issues identified a range of
other topics consistent with the other reviews of the literature.

These comprised the conceptualisation associated with the AFC model,
implementation, development, assessment, and challenges and opportunities associated with the AFCs. Torku et al.'s (2021) commentary highlighted the localised nature of the AFC model and its community focus,
sometimes underpinned by a national policy framework associated with
positive or healthy ageing. Plouffe et al. (2016) observed that implementation was a weakness in the AFC model, with weak global rollout compared
to UNWHO strategies on health. Part of the problem of implementation
relates to its model of development, which is essentially a hybrid one. For
example, the initial stimulus for the AFC initiative for a locality comes from
the top down, and usually made by a political leader or another champion.
But it also requires a community, bottom-up approach to engaging local

communities and herein lies the hybrid conundrum: what should the balance of each AFC be, in terms of governance with a top-down approach and a bottom-up model in terms of the implementation process? Torku et al. (2021) suggested that the strength of this hybrid approach may be in the ability to engage with other agendas, such as the repurposing of urban environments to make them more accessible, along with adapting cities to become more multigenerational in how they are designed. Torku et al. (2021) also highlighted how the development of AFC schemes depend upon a governance structure that reflects the top-down and bottom-up approaches, with a collaborative ideology at its heart that spans a more decentralised community-focused model in some localities. Steering committees were also seen as a key success factor in implementation, and these often reflect the enthusiasm of promoters of the scheme.

In terms of assessment, a variety of toolkits have been developed that also embrace micro-methodologies, such as the use of pedometers for physical exercise and the use of GPS to monitor older people's movement and activity (also see Almeida 2016's use of a tool to assess the walkability of an age-friendly environment). A large proportion of the published research has focused on the perception of age-friendliness using qualitative and quantitative analysis and mixed methods. For example, Bhuyan et al.'s (2020) analysis of the meaning of age-friendly neighbourhoods identified a series of themes, including a sense of place, inclusiveness, the social environment, the physical environment and safety. Bhuyan et al. (2020) concluded that these themes were multi-layered, particularly in terms of the respondents' daily lived experiences. Van Hoof et al.'s (2021) analysis of the Hague as an age-friendly city highlighted the heterogeneity of older people's lived experiences, with important implications for policy-makers. These studies typically need to align with the baseline data that WHO requires all AFCs to collect at the outset to help monitor and assess progress towards AFC objectives and policies in terms of the eight domains.

Other studies such as Sánchez-González et al.'s (2020) review article, have examined AFC interventions from a psychosocial perspective. According to Sanchez-Gonzales et al., a psychosocial perspective focuses on 'processes that are precisely designed, planned and executed in order to influence the personal and community wellbeing of the population, by means of changes in values, policies, programmes, allocation of resources, power differentials and cultural norms' (Sánchez-González et al. 2020: 4–5). The study illustrated ways in which to make alterations to the daily lives of older people: these span the use of assistive technologies and devices, safety measures, information and education, and social interventions such as empowerment to become more engaged with AFCs and training. Among the positive changes commonly observed in AFCs, as

Sánchez-González et al. (2020) noted, was city-based bus travel becoming more age-friendly, adaptations to the home environment and enhanced perceptions of open space in terms of improved accessibility and safety. Even so, Plouffe et al. (2016) argued that the WHO checklist of age-friendly criteria does not adequately capture the diversity of older adults and their communities. But the checklist still forms the basis of most research studies that seek to assess progress towards age-friendliness. Nevertheless, Torku et al. (2021) offer a very pointed assessment of the challenges and opportunities facing AFCs, and these span political, financial, social and physical domains, with the physical domain involving the characteristics of the environment.

Complementing these reviews is a growing range of grey literature that comprises unpublished or published research disseminated non-commercially, such as government reports, policy statements and other position papers that exists typically on the World Wide Web. Among the most widely cited are the studies by WHO although many other policy documents exist, both guides to the creation of AFCs in different localities and manuals and guides of how to become age-friendly (WHO 2007a,b). Glasgow City Council (2015) provided an example of the community consultation process associated with the preliminary stages of becoming age-friendly. The WHO (2015) guide has been widely used as a how-to guide focused on the three principles of equity, accessibility of the physical environment and inclusivity, and includes case studies. In contrast, Handler's (2014) alternative age-friendly guide, drawn from an urban design perspective, looks at tools that can be used to engage the community. The guide also reviews all aspects of the physical environment, including inclusive urban design, observing the decline in age-friendly elements in the UK. Among some of the contextual factors noted by Handler (2014) that impact the creation of age-friendly environments were the following:

- a third of all people over 65 years of age will fall over once a year outside of their home; half of all people over 65 years of age face problems getting outdoors
- a quarter of older people are affected by urinary incontinence
- older people are more likely to be dissatisfied with their neighbourhood than with their home environment
- 12% of people over 65 feel cut off from society
- around 50% of people aged over 75 are fearful of leaving their homes after dark
- almost 25% of older people suffer from urinary incontinence, but the number of public toilets dropped by 40% between 2004 and 2014 (and the situation has continued to deteriorate since then). Saner (2021)

suggests that this has risen to an estimated loss of 50% of toilets in the period 2011–2021. This contributes to a reliance on familiar routes where access to a toilet is known about, causing the phenomenon of 'bladder leash', which tethers people to a limited activity space near to home

- there is a lack of suitable places to sit outdoors that are resting places, and that are safe to use, comfortable and function as a rest stop
- there is growing sensitivity to pavement design and the gradient of streets and evenness of surfaces that can contribute to falls or present obstructions/obstacles.

Handler also offers advice on how to address some of these problems along with an age-friendly checklist that can be read alongside the WHO's 84 rec-ommendations on what needs to be done to make a city age-friendly. But as Handler (2014: 63) noted, checklists can be self-limiting, as

> *there is always a risk that in [sic] focusing on what is fundamental, basic, essential and/or actionable means leaving out what is less obvious or more complex – concerns and issues that are less obviously acted upon. In this way, the practice of reading and ticking boxes can be, not just self-limiting, but can also encourage a bare minimum of compliance.*

Handler's (2014) study is instructive because it shows that urban design will often require retrofitting, modifying and adapting to meet older peo-ple's changing needs, as their mobility changes, for example. The guide also offers many excellent examples of where changes have been made that make a difference. It provides many refreshing ideas on collaboration to bridge the public–private spaces within cities and how to adopt small innovations that overcome barriers in the physical environment. In particular, it high-lights methodologies that can be employed to help places become more age-friendly, including community audits, walking alongside people in the urban environment to observe barriers and solutions, co-designing the environment, participatory research and engagement methods, and civic engagement. Other studies include Tinker and Ginn (2015), which reviewed the journey that London was on towards becoming age-friendly and what additional actions were needed. Further, Age Friendly Bristol (2019) advanced agendas such as the notion of making businesses age-friendly, presenting a useful example of a business-friendly guide. The City of Unley (2019) developed an auditing approach for the products and services of businesses seeking to become age-friendly, which used self-certification via a checklist method; it focused on customer service, marketing, ambience, design and accessibility.

Shannon (2018) provided a review of the implementation of the age-friendly programme in Ireland using secondary data and semi-structured interviews. Initial funding was deemed critical in the implementation and success of the scheme in Ireland. The Public Health Agency of Canada (2012) developed guidance on how to turn a plan into action, focusing on governance (from establishing an age-friendly committee to creating an action plan and communicating the process to the local community). The Public Health Agency of Canada (2012) Age-Friendly Communities Evaluation Guide also outlined how to measure progress on each of the domains within the WHO framework, and what types of measures to use, after establishing the baseline study with key data and indicators. In contrast, other more generic studies such as Standards Research (2019) examined Canada's ageing society and the future development needs associated with that in terms of employment, the home and the community, addressing cross-cutting themes such as equity and engagement. Age-friendly schemes were also referred to in the study along with other public-sector-directed initiatives. Many of these issues have been revisited in the academic literature on AFCs, and we now highlight some of the most significant themes of relevance to this study.

Thematic analysis of the AFC literature

Nykiforuk et al. (2017) examined the role of policy influencers in Alberta, Canada in promoting physical activity and the outdoors as part of an age-friendly strategy to engage more people in the local community. Three key themes emerged from their study: a need for public engagement; the importance of comprehensive planning; and the need to prioritise the needs of older people. Russell et al.'s (2019) study is indicative of many of the more thematic reviews of AFCs and the research literature and is based on a qualitative analysis of age-friendly initiatives in 11 communities in one province of Canada. It questions these programmes' long-term stability and their over-reliance upon volunteers in relation to the administrative burden of the process and draws attention to the existence of an implementation gap. The physical environment has been a significant focus of attention, especially given the positive-ageing and active-ageing tenets of many age-friendly policy interventions before the age-friendly paradigm was developed. But promoting outdoor physical activity and passive leisure pursuits, as Peng and Maing (2021) suggest, may have ramifications where the climate is hotter and given the propensity for urban heat islands to exist in highly urbanised areas. These issues are likely to be exacerbated by climate change, making older citizens more vulnerable to health problems in the use of outdoor green spaces. An emergent theme that is growing in significance in terms of the age-friendly agenda is the application of technology. For example, van Hoof and Marston's (2021) review of technology observed that this was a major omission from the WHO criteria, as societies are moving towards smart technology, which has potential applications to help those dependent on long-term care (also see Kavšek et al. 2021).

Planning, as both a subject and a practice, also remains one of the vital elements that can help in the design, adaptation and creation of more age-friendly places and spaces. Handler (2014) outlined some of the most commonly incorporated principles of urban design, which included: 'wide and flat tarmac footways; easy transition at level changes; clear, simple and easily visible and understandable signage; frequent, warm supportive seating; well-maintained and open public toilets' (Handler 2014: 55); these facilities need to be maintained and functioning in order to be accessible. In some visionary locales, more innovative provision has been incorporated, such as play equipment suitable for older people's needs. Handler also looks at visionary principles in planning of flexible borrowing (or appropriation) of facilities for specific programmes of events that meet older people's needs so they fill a gap in provision. The Community Toilet Provision Scheme is one such innovation, where businesses pledge to make their toilets free and accessible to the general public (including non-customers).

Scott (2021) introduced the widely used lifetime neighbourhood concept as a challenge to the planning profession, arguing that 'it is vital to move beyond considering the role of planning in contributing towards maintaining physical and mental health, and to question how we can make better places that enable citizens to live lives to the full and to flourish' (Scott 2021: 459). This is conceptualised as ageing well in place at a localised level. The problem in the UK is that citizens' longevity is not being matched by the well-being of those citizens, as long life is often accompanied by poor health and issues such as disability (see Page and Connell 2022 for more detail), and so engagement is problematic. The age-friendly paradigm also means planning needs to be more participative, as Murtagh et al. (2022) highlight, and we will return to this later.

Perhaps one of the most useful overviews of these themes, and one that provides a more holistic understanding of the age-friendly model and what is required to make it a success (as well as factors that inhibit that success), is Menec and Brown's (2018) analysis of facilitating factors and barriers. Menec and Brown (2018) summarised, from 13 studies, the enablers of AFCs, as shown in Table 2.3. What Table 2.3 illustrates is that there are three specific enablers: multi-level leadership, effective governance and forming diverse partnerships to progress the AFC agenda. These are associated with a range of facilitating factors as well as barriers. Menec and Brown (2018) also identified process-related factors, which included the involvement of local older people as well as constructing an action plan

Table 2.3 Summary of enablers and processes

Themes	Subthemes	Facilitators	Barriers
Enablers	Multilevel leadership and common vision	• Leadership and commitment at national/regional and local level • Coherence between national/regional and local vision • National/regional ageing strategy • Champion	• Change in policy direction • Turnover in leadership
	Effective governance and management	• Diverse steering committee that includes older adults • High-level government representation on steering committee • Staff • Clearly defined roles and responsibilities	• Lack of volunteers/ volunteer burnout • Lack of skills
	Diverse partnerships	• Intergovernmental • Intersectoral • Public-private sector • With researchers	• Conflict between groups • Competing interests • Lack of common objectives
Processes	Identifying priorities based on older adults' involvement Developing an action plan that corresponds to identified needs	• Acknowledging/building on existing resources • Entrenching action plan in local services • Integrating age-friendliness with other initiatives/ strategies • Promoting and raising awareness of age-friendliness • Fostering public support for age-friendly initiatives	• Lack of funding • Lack of common approach/criteria

Note. Facilitators could also be presented as barriers and vice versa. They are listed here in the way in which they were most commonly described in the literature (e.g. the literature tended to highlight the lack of volunteers as a barrier, rather than having volunteers as a facilitator).
Source: Menec and Brown (2018: 12)

based on research that maps to identifiable needs. This study added one additional level of complexity: the existence of contextual factors, some of which we have already highlighted. Contextual factors include the political will and motivation to develop the AFC scheme in a locality as well as the critical distinction between whether the community in question is urban or rural or combines a mix of these environments. Fiscal constraints on delivering the planned AFC, the importance of an ageing demographic in the locality and its significance in political decision-making were all important contextual factors. Whether or not the locality had a history of policy initiatives and actions on ageing-related issues was also deemed important. For example, in the UK context, McGarry (2019) outlined how an Audit Commission (2008) report on ageing strategies had led to a series of funded work programmes on ageing in specific localities. These created examples of best practice, and in the case of Manchester (and other localities), helped provide some of the groundwork on ageing and social policy development that would underpin AFC development. Woo and Choi (2022) reaffirmed the importance of political motivation in the decision of communities to seek WHO AFC Network membership but also the failure to translate the enthusiasm into implementation that was attributed to lacklustre performance of political will. Given the significance of these enablers and constraining factors, attention now turns to the underpinning philosophy of how the AFC is operationalised with the local community; namely, the type of community development model it uses.

The policy context for age-friendly development: The application of the community development model

There has been a substantial growth in policy research that examines the concept of community development. Among the reviews of the field (e.g. Craig et al. 2011; Phillips and Pittman 2009; Eversley 2019), most studies acknowledge it was a product of the post-war period (Kenny et al. 2017). Yet as a concept it embraces a wide range of views and approaches as well as political stances that can negate consensus due to the diverse philosophical stances. In its definition of community development in the 1950s, as a 'process designed to create conditions of economic and social progress for the whole community with its active participation' (United Nations 1955: 6, cited in Gilchrist and Taylor 2011), the United Nations identified the fundamental principles of the concept. In essence, it is about how practitioners and individuals/groups help members of a community to articulate their needs. Although various definitions and theoretical frameworks exist, some of the core themes are empowerment, power (and how to transform the status quo) and the agents of community development (e.g. practitioners and third parties external to the community, leader(s) of different community interests who animate and facilitate the community development process). The process of community development has a place-specific focus at a neighbourhoods or larger spatial unit such as a district with a focus on improving the population's lot in the community (e.g. through poverty alleviation schemes), and so it is ideally suited to the AFC model. As a philosophy, community development has a salience with how people place different meanings and values on their neighbourhood at the micro scale, along with the psychological and sociological concepts of connectedness, community and place identity (which, in this case, also underpin the AFC movement). Community development also spans associated fields such as human and community rights, as we have illustrated in terms of the antecedents of the AFC movement such as the right to the city. From an applied perspective, community development in the AFC model is operationally focused on how to engage and connect with a specific segment of the community – the ageing population and other stakeholders, including businesses. Key concepts in this context are collaboration, public participation, listening to different voices of the community and how these voices are integrated into community plans.

For the purist, the specific community development model with which the AFC development process most closely aligns is a blend of community-based participatory research and the participatory planning model. The former is theoretically classified as a bottom-up approach that is designed to elicit community responses in order to identify the needs and issues which community members and community-based organisations and stakeholders identify as significant, and to then effect change. Within the AFC model, this still requires leadership from the AFC initiative and so action from the top down may be needed so that information-gathering and the research process can begin at the community level. In contrast, participatory planning is a specific planning approach that seeks (perhaps idealistically) to engage the entire community around strategic management issues (e.g. how to manage municipal responses to ageing). Whilst participation is the main driver, it is implemented as a top-down approach in many settings, in engaging the community using community research methods such as focus groups, public meetings, leaflets, the media and surveys) to pursue a public consultation process. One important consideration here is also the digital divide that exists in many communities, with lower levels of digital skills among older citizens affecting the reach of the consultation process.

Reviews of the community development approach used by AFCs, such as King et al. (2020), use a bottom-up approach methodology to capture community voices. King et al. (2020) advocate community participatory research as part of a wider engagement and empowerment of older people to help them feel a greater sense of participation in the community, although the extent of participation encouraged is also a major area of debate. As King et al. (2020) explain, when a citizen science model is adopted, it can comprise three distinct approaches (a *for the people approach*; a *with the people approach* and a *by the people approach*), with *by the people* seen as a key partnership approach by all stakeholders. Other reviews of the community planning approach, such as Murtagh et al. (2022), highlight the challenge of shaping the city (or place) cognitively for an ageing population and the existing inability of the functional government to do this at a municipal level. Murtagh et al. (2022: 63) highlight the key challenge of bringing together 'functional perspectives (being active), subjectivities (how older people feel) and adaptive processes (an ability to cope with lifecourse change)', and how policies are developed to create place-based programmes. Here the priority, particularly due to the financial imperatives, is to keep older people living independently in their homes for as long as possible, which accords with what most older people want. Murtagh et al. (2022) used the case study of Age-Friendly Belfast to illustrate how the application of the participatory planning model was used and how engagement by planners was a weakness, given their focus on the economic development model in public planning. Here the normative culture of planners around urban management and transportation meant knowledge and data collected from ageing people needed to be fitted to the planning context to evidence the need for service changes. This strategy even included the use of older 'mystery shoppers', who posed as service users to collect information in order to disprove the transportation planners' arguments on the accessibility of services.

Some critics also point to the limited range of older people who engage in participatory planning exercises, as more affluent older people participated in the Age-Friendly Belfast example, which did not reflect the spatial concentration of older people from different demographics in more deprived neighbourhoods. In response, Age-Friendly Belfast now prioritises poverty reduction, including meaningful work for older people. Similar mismatches existed between the ambitions of Northern Ireland's Active Ageing Strategy and civil servants' lack of clarity about how this strategy should be mapped to age-friendly initiatives to help people live longer in their community. Northern Ireland is also an interesting example, given that the devolved government promoted age-friendly initiatives across that entire country, a theme we shall return to later on in the book. We now move on to consider some of the models of implementation of the AFC model at different spatial scales, drawing upon some of the most frequently cited examples in the research literature.

Global models of AFC implementation

Given the scale and growth of the AFC project globally, it is interesting to observe how some countries have endorsed this model and then rolled it out on a systematic basis, although such examples are in the minority. In the main, AFCs are a permissive form of initiative, adopted at a local or regional level, and so their implementation remains a voluntary activity that ultimately is dependent upon the motivation and inspiration of political leaders or individuals who choose to champion the idea. Two countries that much of the literature and practitioners point to are Canada and Ireland (see Plouffe and Kalache 2011).

Canada

Canada is one of the pioneers of the age-friendly movement, as Plouffe and Kalache (2011) highlight, as its Public Health Agency provided the WHO with funding to support the Age Friendly Cities Guide (WHO 2007a). Plouffe and Kalache (2011) illustrated the ageing trajectory of the country; the proportion of the population aged over 65 was set to grow from 14% (2011) to 23% by 2036. Yet like in Ireland, some rural provinces had significant concentrations of over 65-year-olds in 2011, such as Nova Scotia, where this group made up 21% of the population compared to 15% in the country's urban areas. The lead provided by Public Health Canada also saw the creation in 2007 of the Federal /Provincial/Territorial Ministers Responsible for Seniors (2007) report, *Age-Friendly Rural and Remote Communities: A Guide*, which established the roadmap of how to make rural communities more age-friendly. The Canadian approach to the age-friendly concept is to target communities, especially smaller towns and villages, using a community development paradigm. Plouffe and Kalache (2011) provide a detailed review of the evolution of the Canadian model, and the developments in Canada have generated a significant number of research studies that examine different facets of the age-friendly experience. Although there are many examples of age-friendly cities being developed (e.g. see Garon et al. 2014 for an analysis of Quebec), the rural examples offer many interesting insights, as Menec et al. (2013) found in the case of Manitoba. As Plouffe and Kalache (2011) observed, the successes in Canada included a total of 560 communities in eight Canadian provinces engaging in age-friendly initiatives from 2007 to 2011. Key success factors included the support from the provincial and federal government in terms of fostering partnerships and policy instruments. The WHO Age-Friendly Network database lists a number of the Canadian communities that have also joined the WHO network as an indication of the diversity and scale of communities joining; this is illustrated in Table 2.4, which shows the range of those involved, from very small communities through to large urban areas.

Table 2.4 Age-friendly communities in Canada

Place	Province	Population Size	% of Population Over 60	Year Joined
Ajax	Ontario	121,780	16	2020
Stonewall	Manitoba	13,000	20	2018
West Vancouver	British Columbia	42,695	25	2012
Ville de Québec (Quebec City)	Quebec	531,902	21	2018
City of Oshawa	Ontario	170,095	23	2019
Rothesay	New Brunswick	11,659	44	2019
Longueuil	Quebec	246,152	24	2019
Kinnokimaw	Saskatchewan	250	75	2019
Municipality of St Charles	Ontario	1,269	30	Not listed
City of Maple Ridge	British Columbia	82,256	22	2019
Ville De Dieppe	New Brunswick	25,384	20	Not listed
City of Temiskaming Shores	Ontario	9,920	30.7	Not listed
Regional Municipality of Wood Buffalo	Alberta	111,687	6.6	2016
Stonewall Municipality of Rockwood	Manitoba	13,000	20	2018
City of Thorold	Ontario	18,000	22	2018
City of Fredericton	New Brunswick	60,000	24	Not listed
Ville de Beresford	New Brunswick	4,288	33.6	2018
City of Cornwall	Ontario	48,786	16.4	2018
St Thomas	Ontario	40,000	20	2018
Kativik	Quebec	13,683	6	2018
Elgin County	Ontario	50,069	30	2018
Sarnia	Ontario	71,594	24	2018
City of Greater Sudbury	Ontario	166,130	26.7	2018
Elliot Lake	Ontario	10,741	46.4	2018

Place	Province	Population Size	% of Population Over 60	Year Joined
Municipalité du Canton de Bedford	Quebec	663	29	2018
Town of Niagara on the Lake	Ontario	17,511	41	Not listed
Corporation of the County of Brant	Ontario	36,707	26.08	2018
Municipality of Saanich	British Colombia	11,400	28	2006
Saint-Isidore-de-Clifton	Quebec	674	45	2017
Brantford	Ontario	97,000	19	2017
Municipality of Port Hope	Ontario	16,000	25	2017
Saskatoon	Saskatchewan	253,000	13	2017
Pelham	Ontario	17,110	29	2017
Montreal	Quebec	1,780,000	15	2017
La Ville de Cap-Santé	Quebec	3,417	16	2017
La Pêche	Quebec	7,619	22	2017
MRC des Basques	Quebec	8,860	27	2017
Municipalité de Saint-Isidore	Quebec	3,017	14	2017
Ville de Saint-Basile-Le-Grand	Quebec	16,944	20	2017
Shawinigan	Quebec	50,000	22.8	2017
Chertsey	Quebec	5,000	30	2017
Orangeville	Ontario	27,975	16.37	2017
MRC de La Matanie	Quebec	21,00	25	2017
MRC du Domaine-du-Roy	Quebec	30,000	17	2017
Ville de Notre-Dame-des-Prairies	Quebec	9,700	28	2017
Brampton	Ontario	603,346	9	2017
Duparquet	Quebec	575	30	2016
Mont Saint-Grégoire	Quebec	2,995	20	2016

(*Continued*)

Table 2.4 (Continued)

Place	Province	Population Size	% of Population Over 60	Year Joined
Grande-Vallée	Quebec	1,089	40	2016
Saint-Joseph-de-Beauce	Quebec	4,853	20	2016
Notre-Dame-de-Monts	Quebec	830	55	2016
Municipalité de la Maraza	Quebec	1,040	37	2016
Municipalité des Bergeronnes	Quebec	695	29	2016
Saint-Jean-Baptiste	Quebec	3,250	30	2016
Saint-Jacques-le-Mineur	Quebec	1,660	19.76	2016
Saint-Gabriel-Lalemant	Quebec	785	29	2016
Ville D'Otterburn Park	Quebec	8,397	16.6	2016
Municipalité de Saint-Thomas	Quebec	677	37	2016
Grosses-Roches	Quebec	400	50	2016
Dégelis	Quebec	2,980	30	2016
Fortierville	Quebec	706	25	2016
Municipalité de Sainte-Eulalie	Quebec	900	25	2016
Municipalité de Saint-Edmond-les-Plaines	Quebec	385	53	2016
Municipalité de Saint-Jean-de-Brébeuf	Quebec	368	28	2016
Municipalité de Saint-Stanislas-de-Kostka	Quebec	1,585	35	2016
Municipalité de Saint-Guy	Quebec	82	65	2016
Saint-Jude	Quebec	1,241	1.2	2016
Verchères	Quebec	5,800	20	2016
Lanoraie	Quebec	4,570	?	2016
Bedford	Quebec	2,575	21.8	2016

Place	Province	Population Size	% of Population Over 60	Year Joined
French River	Ontario	2,500	30	Not listed
Surrey	British Columbia	493,200	12.6	Not listed
Summerside	Prince Edward Island	15,000	27	Not listed
Calgary	Alberta	1,613,500	16	Not listed
Peterborough	Ontario	121,721	29.8	2016
Wood Buffalo	Alberta	125,032	4.9	2016
Chatham-Kent	Ontario	103,600	25	2016
Toronto	Ontario	2,808,000	19.8	2016
Portage la Prairie	Manitoba	12,996	17.5	2012
Windsor	Ontario	210,981	21.6	2012
Guelph	Ontario	121,622	15	2014
Hamilton	Ontario	236,917	24	2015
Moncton	New Brunswick	69,074	34.4	Not listed
Whitby	Ontario	134,875	25.8	2014
Hearst	Ontario	5,070	24	2012
Kingston	Ontario	123,000	18	2011
Sault Ste. Marie	Ontario	75,000	20	2012
Waterloo	Ontario	113,520	13	2011
Welland	Ontario	52,293	25	2010
London	Ontario	266,151	21	2010
Edmonton	Alberta	817,498	18	2010
Thunder Bay	Ontario	108,360	24	2011
Port Colborne	Ontario	19,000	22	2014
Ottawa	Ontario	100,000	17	2011

Source: Extracted from the WHO Age-Friendly Communities database (https://extranet.who.int/agefriendlyworld/who-network/)

At a national scale, Canada's Ministry of Health was very supportive of the development, providing guidance for communities on how to navigate the process of turning these ambitions into reality. The Government of Canada's 'how-to guides', such as its *Age-Friendly Communities Implementation Guide* (Public Health Agency of Canada 2012), mapped out how to move from a strategy and action plan to implementation. Additional developments included a pan-Canada age-friendly network to connect age-friendly communities, the development of age-friendly training in private sector companies and the creation of Age-Friendly Business Guides in specific locales (e.g. the Age-Friendly London Network, Canada in 2016, which created the *Age-Friendly Business Resource Guide*, https://www.informationlondon.ca/uploads/contentdocuments/afb%20resource%20guide_final.pdf).

Ireland

Ireland, like Canada, has adopted a national approach towards age-friendly activity and has created an impressive infrastructure to support its ambitions, as is evident from the guidance on its website (https://agefriendlyireland.ie). McDonald et al. (2018) reviewed Ireland's development and progress towards becoming an age-friendly country, which can be traced to the launch of the Age-Friendly Cities and Counties programme in 2010, which covers each of the country's 31 local authorities. As McDonald et al. (2018) observed, this was a major achievement as it was developed amidst the background of national austerity and a financial crisis. The leadership of the age-friendly initiative was funded by a philanthropic foundation on a fixed-term basis to help establish an independent think tank – the Ageing Well Network, which created the momentum and focus needed to begin Ireland's age-friendly journey in 2007. The key challenge facing the age-friendly initiative was not necessarily the volume of the ageing population over 65 years of age – which, in 2016, was 637,000, equivalent to 13.4% of the total population (expected to rise to 1:4, or 25% of the population). Instead, the issue was the geographical distribution of the population, 40% of whom live in larger cities, 31% in smaller towns and 27% in a diversity of rural areas that span semi-urban to remoter rural areas. This illustrates the challenge already noted above, that one size does not fit all in designing age-friendly programmes. In addition, McDonald et al. (2018) highlighted the issues around urban–rural differences. Proportionally more older people lived in rural areas; 87% of older adults owned their own homes; 11% of the population aged over 65 were in employment; car ownership was low among older people (e.g. 20% of those in rural and 33% of those in urban areas had no access to cars) along with lower levels of access to the internet. Among the key achievements in the early stages of the age-friendly development were two national programmes: (a) Older People Remaining at Home, and (b) Age-Friendly Towns, which showed that small changes could make major differences to the local environment (e.g. provision of seats and benches and improvements to pedestrian crossings). These programmes were complemented by the national government strategy on ageing in 2013.

Age-Friendly Ireland (AFI) replaced the Ageing Well Network in 2013 and its scope and successes were significant in transforming the thinking about ageing in Ireland. Among some of the key metrics that AFI cite are that 20,000 people have engaged in the consultation process across the

16 counties since the age-friendly initiative began; a further 19,500 have engaged with it through household interviews; a network has been created of local-level partnerships and alliances that are older-people-focused, in order to implement the age-friendly programmes so they are tailored to local needs. A comprehensive set of guides have been created by AFI that span: planning; seating; car parking; primary care; the suitability of current housing, and ways to make adaptations to housing or enabling citizens to move to more suitable age-friendly accommodation (called rightsizing); hospital care, the walkability of the urban environment; public services; issues around loneliness; and an age-friendly business toolkit (see https://agefriendlyireland.ie). The Age-Friendly Ireland (2021) guidance on housing illustrates the type of thinking the guides offer; it lists the key features of an age-friendly home. Such a home

> *is well connected to local amenities, is easy to approach and enter; is connected to the outdoors; is easy to move about in; has accessible and adaptable toilets and bathrooms; has a guest bedroom; has easy to use fittings and fixtures; is energy and cost efficient and has good security and technology systems.* (Age-Friendly Ireland 2021: 4)

One final example of an initiative in a city that has developed into a city-region model, often cited as an early exemplar of the age-friendly approach, is Manchester.

Manchester

Manchester, in north-west England, is the UK's fifth-largest city and around a third of its population are from minority ethnic groups. The city has a population of around 500,000 and a wider urban conurbation includes around 2.7 million people. Around 10.5% of the city's population are aged over 65 years of age, which is below the England and Wales average of 16.9%, but this does not reflect the significant socio-economic difficulties which the ageing population in the city and wider region face. As McGarry (2019) outlined, the older population is polarised between the more affluent, who have migrated out of former inner-Manchester districts, and those they left behind in those districts, who are more vulnerable and face greater levels of multiple deprivation. Those living in highly urbanised districts are subject to higher levels of disadvantage (facing premature death, i.e. earlier than age 75) compared to the residents of other English local authorities. Even those older people who live beyond age 75 in Manchester face poorer health and levels of disability according to McGarry (2019), making ageing a social issue that is interconnected with many other agendas in municipal management including poverty, social exclusion, health, housing, social care, planning, transportation and environmental quality, areas that are reflected in the WHO's eight domains.

Manchester is an interesting example, as was highlighted earlier in Table 2.1, in that it is an example of a city that had an existing history of interest in ageing as a policy issue in the form of its Valuing Older People programme (McGarry 2019). From the early 1990s, Manchester began to challenge the existing local-authority model of thinking about ageing as a social responsibility that was predominantly focused on the 'social care' paradigm', as set out in Chapter 1. McGarry (2019) outlined the initial age-friendly work that had indicated that most ageing people in the city of Manchester did not receive social care from the municipal bodies and that a more inclusive and engaging approach was needed to overcome existing social exclusion in service provision beyond social care. Key milestones in Manchester's age-friendly journey in the new millennium included the 2009 Manchester Ageing Study 2010–2019, which closely aligned itself to the WHO AFC model, and the city joined the WHO network in 2009. As an age-friendly city, it has attracted large-scale funding to pursue that agenda and has successfully rolled out an initiative to create the first age-friendly region – Age-Friendly Greater Manchester – by placing greater focus on expanding the economic participation of older people and adopting a neighbourhood approach as the central feature of its engagement strategy with communities. The political support the initiative has generated over many years has helped to embed age-friendly thinking across all areas of the local authorities working on age-friendly matters and it remains a beacon that many other age-friendly communities look to, seeking to understand the success factors underpinning its implementation and development.

Summary

From these three short examples, it is evident that momentum, political support, funding and a strategic view of ageing from the AFC movement have helped localities to engage with the age-friendly agenda. The considerable growth in the research literature on the age-friendly theme has meant that this chapter has only provided headline themes associated with the key strands of thinking in this book, as the age-friendly literature now spans many disciplines and extends across science and technology, social science and humanities. The diversity of approaches and theoretical frameworks adopted towards the age-friendly theme make any synthesis partial, as many of the review articles on the age-friendly domain demonstrate. The literature is now becoming more disparate and at times quite eclectic. Much of it is experience-based or reflective of the progress, achievements, and limitations facing localities, with the typical academic traits of lengthy action lists of what needs to be done to make things better. It is evident that a greater level of pragmatism in the interpretations and critiques of age-friendly progress is needed in order to recognise that this is not a core function of local government. Consequently, whilst elements of local government functions straddle ageing, despite the success of the age-friendly model from the WHO, it needs to be acknowledged that it is not a panacea for addressing the structural problems of ageing in society. Instead, it is a step towards improving the environments and societal interactions that older people encounter, in a long journey towards a more normalised experience whereby ageing is not stigmatised in society. The age-friendly movement helps explain to different stakeholders how their involvement in communities can be incorporated in order to achieve strategic objectives in managing an ageing population.

Although academic conceptualisation, theorisation and analysis may help communicate with other academics, we should not forget that the latter are in many cases bystanders in this process (apart from where they are working with organisations on research projects that feed into age-friendly actions directly). Therefore, commentary and critiques of specific locales and communities and programmes have helped build up a considerable, if overly descriptive, knowledge base that needs greater synthesis and a comparative frame to scale up the observations on the basis of which assessments are made. Some of the recent analyses of age-friendly programmes globally confirm that more comparative studies will help to understand the nuances of the experiences of the age-friendly model. It is also apparent that the model needs further refinement to embrace the significance of technology and its relationship to helping older people live longer at home in greater comfort and safety. Van Hoof et al. (2021) also argued for a greater emphasis on technology across the eight domains of the WHO model based on research from gerontechnology, and the developments in smart technology which show the potential to help with daily living in terms of homes and the physical environment. The expansion of smartphones and apps and smart sensors may also help break down social isolation in older age and help enable self-management of older people's health. But as Van Hoof et al. (2021) highlight, the digital divide in the UK still poses challenges in terms of the digital poverty that some older people face, along with the issue of their skills in terms of using technology.

From the review of the age-friendly literature highlighted in this short summary and from a wider reading of the literature, it is evident that it is timely to consider experiences by country and how these can be disaggregated at the city and community level. In other words, by adopting a country-based approach, broader themes and comparative experiences can be understood in order to address the research questions posed in Chapter 1. For this reason, attention now turns to the primary and secondary research elements of the study within a UK context.

3 Developing age-friendly communities in the UK

Perspectives from practice

Introduction

The development of an age-friendly society in the United Kingdom has largely been shaped by the public sector (and to a lesser degree the voluntary sector), which is sometimes referred to as public administration. Pollitt (2010: 292) described public administration as being unified by 'its subject – the state, the public sector and public realm – not its aims, theories or methods. It is in effect a community of interest.' This quotation aptly describes the context in which age-friendly developments occur. Although there are semantic debates about whether one should look at age-friendly development through a public-sector-management or public-administration lens, each approach has merit, as this chapter explores. For example, a public-sector-management perspective focuses on the way resources and priorities are met by public sector organisations. In contrast, the public-administration approach adopts a broader remit, examining how different interests intersect and coalesce to focus on issues in the public realm (see Chapter 1). The underlying premise in both of these approaches is how the needs of ageing communities are met through public-sector organisations.

The organisations responsible for the management and governance of local communities in the UK comprise a complex array of bodies. As the Local Government Association (LGA) (www.local.gov.uk/) identifies, there are 34 county councils, 181 district, borough or city councils, 59 unitary councils, 33 London boroughs and 34 metropolitan boroughs, complemented by 9000 town and parish councils. The funding for these bodies is largely drawn from several sources: central government grant, council tax and business rates, and services sold by the council (e.g. car parking). The LGA notes that councils offer over 800 different types of services to residents, but their core functions are determined by legislation in terms of their statutory responsibilities. These responsibilities span a wide range of activities such as social care, education, public health,

DOI: 10.4324/9781003319801-3

planning, refuse collection, transport and housing. Councils also perform other non-statutory roles, which vary by area depending on local needs and the political outlook of the council. Activity in these areas is often enabled by legislation that sometimes dates to the Victorian period, and includes managing outdoor space, leisure and recreation provision and cultural resources. In 2013, public health responsibilities in England were transferred from the National Health Service (NHS) to local authorities as part of the Health and Social Care Act (2012), with the broader aim of ensuring that 'functions in relation to the health service are conferred directly on the organisations responsible for exercising them' (https://www.legislation. gov.uk/ukpga/2012/7/notes). This led to the creation of Health and Well-Being Boards at the upper level of local government to provide a strategic oversight of health and well-being in localities, designed to foster health and social care collaboration. This move has created a greater opportunity for age-friendly initiatives to emerge from the healthy-ageing paradigm fostered by local government in the LGA's (2015) guide to healthy ageing with its focus on older people.

To fulfil their roles, councils engage in coordination, policy formulation and interventions to address broad national agendas and more specific local issues and applications. Stephenson (2013) indicated that the two principal challenges for the public sector are: first, democratic accountability, as councils are overseen by elected representatives and thus the political complexion of councils and their priorities may change through time; second, the lack of a single success measure by which council performance can be measured. An added feature is volatility and uncertainty over government funding for councils. Reduced government funding and austerity in public finances (see Johns 2020) have meant that cuts to services have occurred as part of what Flynn (2012) described as both the hollowing-out of the state proper (i.e. the contracting out of, and withdrawal from some areas of activity) and the rise of the regulatory state, where councils are particularly concerned with regulating the activities undertaken by the private sector and those they contract out. Whilst various theorisations interpret these changes, the local state has shrunk its footprint during successive budget cuts, as the following statistics suggest for the period 2010/11 to 2018/20:

- Central government funding in England for councils dropped by 37%
- Cuts to areas of council activity meant that difficult decisions on which areas to cut back, had to be made; e.g. funding for public toilets declined by 48% (see Chapter 2)
- Funding for community development dropped by 58% and for open spaces by 18%.

One response has been the greater forging of partnerships between public-sector bodies, national organisations and third-sector bodies, which have often sought short-term project funding to address specific issues of national importance in the pursuit of resources to deal with local needs. The positive dimension to this is a greater focus on collaboration and cooperation with multiple stakeholders. However, the broader challenge, as Stephenson (2013) acknowledged, in fostering, building and maintaining multi-stakeholder relationships makes the scope of the public sector less manageable. Based on the experiences of age-friendly community creation in the United States, Warner and Zhang (2021) found that where councils had managed to achieve cross-agency collaboration and engagement of older residents a better range of services were provided, and that collaboration was one theme that the WHO model of AFCs should emphasise. Indeed, such partnerships are essential for an organisation seeking to become age-friendly in a given locality because the eight domains of the WHO model span most areas of council work and other stakeholder activity (e.g. businesses and third-sector organisations). Bringing these components together to embark on the age-friendly journey requires a holistic perspective on ageing that an organisation focused on the public realm is well placed to co-ordinate.

Numerous studies of ageing in the UK help us to understand the scope of the challenges communities face with an ageing population, as the following headline statistics show:

- There are 12 million people over 65 years of age living in the UK (19% of the population); by 2032 this will rise to 13 million (22% of the population); by 2040, 40% of the population will be aged 50 or more
- 5.4 million people are aged 75 or over; 1.6 million are aged 85 or over, and over 500,000 people are aged 90 or over; 14,430 are centenarians
- The number of centenarians has increased by 85% in the past 15 years, and it is estimated that there will be over 21,000 centenarians by 2030
- In terms of scale, by 2067 it is estimated that there will be an additional 8.6 million people aged 65 years and over – that is almost the size of London's population in 2020
- In the UK, 'urban areas tend to have a younger, more diverse population' (Hood et al. 2022: 3) hinting at the issue of rural ageing but also the potential invisibility of urban ageing concerns

- The ageing structure of the UK's population means that in 2030 over 1:5 people will be aged 65 or older. The fastest-growing age group is expected to be the over-85-year-olds, who will increase in number from 3.2 million in 2041 to 5.1 million by 2066
- 1:5 people over the age of 60 living at home face conditions that endanger life
- Some 867,000 people over 55 are now renting and spending over 50% of their income on rent
- Average number of years in good health is 60.9 for women and 62.4 for men
- Over 4 million people aged over 65 (40%) are living with a long-term illness such as dementia, cancer, diabetes, heart disease or respiratory disease, blighting their later life and adding a growing burden to the NHS, as some people also have multiple and more complex health conditions that demand long-term care
- The proportion of the older population requiring social-care support has declined through time, especially in the over-80 age group, meaning a greater degree of independent living. However, the number needing social-care support with two or more long-term conditions or limitations on the activities of daily living aged 85 or more has increased. These conditions are normally managed by the NHS. A significant proportion of these conditions are neurological
- Greater participation in physical activity is deemed to be beneficial for helping ameliorate the onset of some of these health conditions, as the healthy-ageing paradigm demonstrates (i.e. greater activity to benefit mental and physical health and to help stem cognitive decline)
- 1:5 over-65-year-olds are living in relative poverty, which is increasing
- 1.3 million over-65-year-olds are living alone, an increase of 67% from 2000 to 2018
- The contribution of the older population as unpaid carers of grandchildren and family saves the state over £132 billion a year
- 1:3 people over age 65 experience at least one fall a year and about half experience multiple falls
- Local authorities with a higher proportion of older people have a lower level of Adult Social Care provision; local authorities with the greatest levels of deprivation are impacted by higher levels of demand from older people for long-term support
- Of the older population, 2 million are affected by material deprivation (i.e. impacting whether families can afford to buy services and essential items or participate in leisure and social activities)

- 'Social deprivation is the most common form of material deprivation for pensioners, with over 90 per cent of materially deprived pensioners lacking a social item (e.g. being able to go on holiday or see friends and family regularly). Very few pensioners lack basic items, such as not being able to have a filling meal each day or not having a warm coat' (Bartlett et al. 2012: 6); social deprivation affects 49% of pensioners to some degree.

Sources: Centre for Ageing Better (2022); Bartlett et al. (2012); Raymond et al. (2021); Age UK (2019); Local Government Association (2018); Hood et al. (2022).

These headline figures show that developing a more age-friendly approach towards service provision requires strategic actions to be taken to help prepare for the changing demographic that is developing. For this reason, attention now turns to the research study, to illustrate how different age-friendly initiatives have been developed and examine their scope and achievements.

The research study

Methodology

In this study, we adopted a qualitative interview approach based on narrative research to investigate the philosophy, development and implementation of age-friendly programmes and practices from the perspective of organisational leaders. A strong driver for this research was to understand the 'why' and 'how' of developing and managing age-friendly initiatives, with a focus on the voices of leaders and managers and recognising their world views, roles and experiences of working in a predominantly participatory and advocacy role. As Creswell and Poth (2013) indicate, where an action agenda for reform is pursued – in this case the age-friendly agenda to improve older people's lives – an advocacy/participatory research method is well suited to capturing the voices of participants. Further, the objective of the age-friendly agenda is to bring about change. Creswell and Poth (2013) identify a narrative research method as being one of the tools that can be used to understand a change agenda. According to Bryman (2008: 713), narrative analysis can be defined as 'an approach to the elicitation and analysis of data that is sensitive to the sense of temporal sequence that people, as tellers of stories about their lives or events around them, detect in their lives and surrounding episodes and inject into their accounts'.

Narrative research

Narrative research is a conversational research technique which aims to gather data through posing open-ended questions which serve to prompt open dialogue between researcher and participant. In its ideal application, narrative analysis can be a setting where the researcher becomes a learner and promotes reflective learning among the participants. The semi-structured interview is used to elicit the narrative and involves a process of mutual understanding between speaker and listener. Narrative inquiry at its heart is focused on the story and events therein, and how this leads to knowledge based on the social contexts and interactions that occur. Contrary to popular belief, as Bryman (2008) notes, narrative techniques are not simply confined to life histories and have been applied within many different contexts, including organisations and public administration. Ospina and Dodge (2005: 144) point to the 'narrative turn' in public administration research and how participants reflect on and interpret their work as employees.

As Webster and Mertova (2007: 2) argue, narrative research 'records human experience through the construction and reconstruction of personal stories; it is well suited to addressing issues of complexity and cultural and human centredness because of its capacity to record and retell those events'. It does so by focusing on longer-term issues that may be a sequence of actions, experiences or human events. Among one of the criticisms of narrative analysis is its subjectivity, but because the aim of our research was to collect stories of age-friendly development from the perspective of those who lead and manage initiatives, it provided a suitable mechanism to hear and interpret stories and construct a narrative about age-friendliness in the UK. Narrative analysis is well suited to advocacy research, whose purpose is to transfer knowledge and communicate new ideas whilst understanding the context in which the issues are reported. From an analytical perspective, the focus in narrative analysis is on critical events or junctures viewed from a human-centred approach, being cognisant of the world views of the participants, without superimposing a predetermined set of assumptions or interpretations to collect the multiplicity of views or voices of the multiple realities that exist. Paschen and Ison (2014) suggest narrative analysis is a useful research approach to use when seeking to understand the interconnections between knowledge, policy and action in applied settings, and as Hollway and Jefferson (2012) suggest, narrative analysis has the benefit of capturing indexicality, which is how people anchor accounts and stories to events. Indexicality, as initially advanced by Garfinkel (1967) from linguistics, highlights how people make sense of their everyday lives as well as the language used, which is context-dependent. The narrative forms an important part of the social communication process, whereby the detail and manner in which the story is told represent the choices made by the storyteller, who often makes free associations between subjects and other phenomena. Whilst the use of a 'question-and-answer' format has a tendency to suppress stories, the skills of the researcher in using prompts to capture the stories and foster the willingness of the participant to tell those stories around several defined aspects may suppress free association. Consequently, we had to make certain compromises, as the participants were working in very busy jobs and a limited amount of time was available in which to capture these narratives.

Epistemologically, we adopt a social constructivism approach to the narratives that accepts that 'human thought, knowledge and action are shaped by language and discourse' (Paschen and Ison 2014: 1084) and recognises that this form of knowledge production is self-reflective and practice focused. One added complexity was that these multiple realities exist in a series of interconnected domains (i.e. how the age-friendly concept is used to address a perceived problem around ageism by politicians and policymakers; how ageing users of services and places experience the tangible and intangible things they consume; and in how businesses and other stakeholders seek to embrace, develop and implement an age-friendly paradigm in their working environments). The narratives captured are by their very nature reflective of Silverman's (2016: 13) characterisation of qualitative research, which 'rarely follows a smooth trajectory from hypothesis to findings. It is an iterative process'. This is because the narratives were sometimes repetitive, were non-linear in terms of the timelines reported and often returned to issues discussed earlier in the interview.

From an interpretivist perspective, the narratives are a complex form of data that offer a rich and deep source from which to interpret what is happening, and to understand highly subjective assessments of the how, why, what and when of age-friendly programmes of work in pursuit of a broader understanding of the multiple realities and layered responses of different stakeholders responsible for age-friendly initiatives. The narrative approach employed here favoured a much deeper and thicker explanatory approach towards social phenomena and is ideally suited to situations where researchers approach the research with no preconceived notions of what causal mechanisms might be at work and what types of data might be important to identifying the specific processes that are in play. Thus, a more iterative process was adopted, where the analysis and interpretation could then draw upon the ideas and concepts in the existing research literature. In this respect, the methodological approach followed here tends to replicate that advocated by O'Mahoney and Vincent (2014) in examining organisations, namely, a literature review drawing on a historical analysis of the literature and phenomenon being studied to highlight more realistic theoretical perspectives. The process of data collection needs to be inclusive and aligned with gathering relevant empirical (quantitative and qualitative) data. The data-analysis stage tends to prioritise epistemology over ontology, generating theory through the data analysis using, in this instance, an abduction approach, which re-describes the observable events provided by interviewees in a more generic sense to seek out regularities in patterns of events in tandem with the theory outlined in the literature. The aim of this approach is to uncover new perspectives, and to make perhaps-unanticipated findings that may also lead to a reconceptualisation of the field.

Research process

The research process is outlined in Figure 3.1. Following the literature review, the UK context was reconstructed from documentary analysis (e.g. council minutes and meetings which established the commitment to becoming age-friendly) along with the large body of grey literature each locality produced as part of the age-friendly process. Reading this documentary evidence helped in understanding the political impetus from individuals wishing to progress this initiative, in contrast to other localities who have not pursued it. Second, collating the list of communities which had embarked on the age-friendly journey, using the Centre for Ageing Better website and supplementary statistical data sources shown in Table 3.1, established the context for the study. Table 3.1 shows that as of January 2021, 33.6% of the UK population were covered by age-friendly schemes. Geographically, the main clusters of AFCs are in north-west England and Northern Ireland, and this reflects the investment by local authorities in those areas (see Figure 3.2). In contrast, London is a different story with various London boroughs taking the lead, as little publicly available information exists since the report by Tinker and Ginn (2015). Much of southern England and most coastal regions are also absent from the age-friendly journey (with several exceptions) along with Scotland, and there have been recent calls for greater action on ageing by Age Scotland (Anon 2022). There is also a greater need, as Chapter 2 highlighted, to examine rural and coastal communities, given the clustering of an ageing demographic in these communities. Northern Ireland stands out as an exemplar of age-friendly progress due to central funding from the devolved assembly to promote the age-friendly agenda. Even so, most interest has been focused on urban areas.

As Figure 3.1 shows, the next stage was an ambitious programme which aimed to interview the majority of age-friendly leads for every locality in the UK; at the time the study was developed (January 2021), there were 41 leads (Table 3.1). A semi-structured interview technique with key

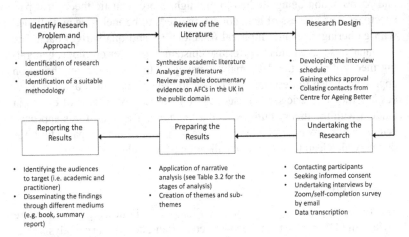

Figure 3.1 The research process used in the study

prompts was selected to understand the multiple realities of age-friendly schemes as well as to allow for a degree of comparative analysis around common themes. The prompt questions were developed based on what was already known and not known about the age-friendly initiative in the UK, so as to prompt, rather than steer the narrative. Ethics approval was sought institutionally to undertake the study and in February 2021, all 41 contacts were contacted according to the ethics protocols. Email contact was made initially, and if interest was expressed, informed consent to participate forms were sent. These had to be returned before an online interview was undertaken via Zoom. The Zoom calls were scheduled to last one hour. The choice of Zoom was necessary due to the Covid pandemic, and so it was the only means by which to communicate with participants to gather their narratives. The advantages and weaknesses of this method were examined using different sources such as James and Busher (2009) and Salmons (2011) in order to understand the use of online video calls and any pitfalls to avoid. Some 23 participants agreed to be interviewed (56%), and a further five (12%) asked to complete the interviews via a semi-structured self-completion survey tool that replicated the interview format and allowed free-flow responses. Most interviews lasted up to an hour, and some ranged between 45 and 90 minutes in duration. All participants agreed to be recorded; the interviews were recorded on Zoom and via a digital voice recording device, which was then downloaded and sent for transcription. On receipt of the transcripts these were checked against

Table 3.1 Key characteristics of the UK's age-friendly communities, January 2021*

Place	County/Province	Population Size	Percentage of population over age 60	Year joined World Health Organization AFC Network
Liverpool City region	Merseyside	153,160	24	2020
London Borough of Hackney	Greater London	279,665	11	2020
Antrim and Newtownabbey	Ulster	142,492	21.4	2020
Fermanagh and Omagh District	Ulster	116,289	21.8	2017
Sheffield	South Yorkshire	578,000	22	2019
Bristol	City of Bristol, Avon	454,200	17.2	2018
Newry, Mourne and Down	Ulster	177,816	19.4	2013
Metropolitan Borough of Sefton	Merseyside	273,790	27	2018
London	Greater London Authority	9,000,630	15.9	2018
Lisburn and Castlereagh	Ulster	141,181	22.3	2018
Ards and North Down Borough	Ulster	159,159	26.4	2018
Cheshire West and Chester Borough	Cheshire	334,000	26.9	2018
Greater Manchester Combined Authority	Greater Manchester	2,812,569	20.8	2018
Coventry	West Midlands	317,000	22	2017
Derry City and Sherbourne	Ulster	28,395	18.7	2013
Isle of Wight	Isle of Wight	140,000	28.3	2016
Salford	Greater Manchester	233,900	11	2016
Sunderland	Tyne and Wear	276,100	20	2015
Liverpool	Merseyside	489,000	14	2014

(Continued)

Table 3.1 (Continued)

Place	County/Province	Population Size	Percentage of population over age 60	Year joined World Health Organization AFC Network
London Borough of Southwark	Greater London	285,300	10.9	2015
Newcastle upon Tyne	Tyne and Wear	279,100	19.4	2014
Glasgow	Lanarkshire	596,550	18.55	2015
Nottingham	Nottinghamshire	331,000	15.5	2014
Manchester	Greater Manchester	575,400	12.7	2010
Belfast	Ulster	280,962	19.3	2014
Stoke-on-Trent	Staffordshire	249,903	21.6	2014
Leeds	West Yorkshire	793,000	20	2014
Brighton and Hove	East Sussex	288,000	17	2013
Wales	Wales	3,500,000	24	Underway; will comprise each locality applying to join the WHO scheme
Armagh	Ulster	200,000	16	2017
York	Yorkshire	209,990	22.3	2019
Oxfordshire	Oxfordshire	687,466	21.9	2016
Birmingham	Greater Birmingham Metropolitan area	1,149,000	18.9	Underway
Trafford	Greater Manchester	237,734	19	2018
London Borough of Sutton	London	206,075	17.7	2020

Melksham	Wiltshire	14,677	38	2018
Hebden	North Yorkshire	4,112	25	2019
Barnsley	West Yorkshire	243,341	21.3	2017
Bolton	Greater Manchester	285,372	22.46	2016
Middlesbrough	North Yorkshire	140,398	16	2018
Torbay	Devon	136,051	32	2019
		Total	Average for	
		24,982,631	England and	
		Covering 37%	Wales 22.5%	

(1) Part of the Greater London data and not disaggregated to the London Boroughs

Source: Centre for Ageing Better contacts list; various sources

* When the list was compiled, there were 41 age-friendly coordinator/contacts on the Centre for Ageing Better website. By April 2022, this had been further updated to include East Lindsey, Yale, Hastings, Wigan, Framlington, Rother, South Lakeland, London Borough of Lewisham and North Yorkshire to recognise 50 localities that were on the age-friendly journey.

1 Antrim and Newtownabbey
2 Ards and North Down
3 Armagh City, Banbridge and Craigavon
4 Banbury
5 Barnsley
6 Belfast
7 Birmingham
8 Bolton
9 Bournemouth
10 Brighton and Hove
11 Bristol
12 Calderdale (added after April 2021)
13 Causeway Coast and Glens
14 Cheshire West
15 Coventry* (was listed in 2021 but not in 2022)
16 Derry City and Strabane
17 East Lindsey (added after April 2021)
18 Fermanagh and Omagh
19 Framlingham (added after April 2021)
20 Glasgow
21 Greater Manchester
22 Hastings (added after April 2021)
23 Hebden Royd
24 Isle of Wight
25 Knowsley (added after April 2021)
26 Leeds
27 Lisburn Castlereagh
28 Liverpool
29 Liverpool City region

30 London
31 London Borough of Hackney
32 London Borough of Lewisham (added after April 2021)
33 London Borough of Southwark
34 London Borough of Sutton
35 Manchester
36 Melksham
37 Mid and East Antrim
38 Mid Ulster (added after April 2021)
39 Middlesbrough
40 Newcastle upon Tyne
41 Newry, Mourne and Down
42 North Yorkshire (added after April 2021)
43 Nottingham
44 Rother (added after April 2021)
45 Salford
46 Sefton
47 Sheffield
48 South Lakeland (added after April 2021)
49 South Tyneside (added after April 2021)
50 Stockport (added after April 2021)
51 Stoke-on-Trent
52 Sunderland
53 Torbay
54 Trafford
55 Wigan
56 Yate (added after April 2021)
57 York

Figure 3.2 Locations of age-friendly communities, 2021 and 2022

the recorded Zoom call. Very few errors were noted; most difficulties arose where clarity was lost on Zoom, but these were infrequent and so relatively accurate records were collected.

One participant covered two council areas, whilst two people engaged in one interview as an officer and line manager. The self-completion tool did collect information that was consistent with the key themes reported in the interviews. The main difference with the self-completed responses was the relative brevity, in some instances, of the responses, though in other cases a lengthy written narrative was provided. Given the ongoing lockdown in the UK, this was deemed to be a very substantial response rate far in excess of many questionnaire surveys, where response rates as low as single digits have been reported. The depth of responses received and the broad coverage of the age-friendly schemes were representative of the range of community types, ranging from large cities to remoter rural areas. For the purposes of assuring confidentiality, we agreed not to name locations or participants' organisations, as this helped to yield very open, frank and deep responses as opposed to simple yes/no replies. This is reflected in the anonymous nature of the quotations that are simply recorded with a number as an identifier. In every instance the participants were very pleased to cooperate and were interested in seeing the results as there had been no UK-wide analysis of how the age-friendly schemes had progressed in their entirety; this reflected the concept of 'practitioners as knowledge producers' (Ospina and Dodge 2005: 152). This interview approach yielded 120,000 words of text, including many rich stories that were well suited to narrative analysis, and a more reflective mode of data capture that suited the participants, with their diverse experiences and knowledge of ageing.

Method of analysis

As a qualitative methodology, narrative analysis was selected, which according to Bryman (2008: 582) is an effective method in terms of finding out how 'people make sense of what happened and to what effect?', 'because stories are nearly always told with a purpose in mind – there is an intended effect'. This approach mapped exactly to the purpose of the study in seeking to gather a range of highly subjective narratives on the evolution and management of, and progress towards implementing age-friendly programmes. Clearly, not all participants were starting from the same calendar date for the scheme's inception (Table 3.1), nor had they had identical organisational models on which to develop their programmes, so this methodology was able to focus on the nuances and idiosyncrasies, as well as how participants sought to make sense of what had happened, why and with what effect in relation to key events. The potential weakness here was in assuming all participants had a good memory or recall, as these factors may give variable results. On the basis of the narratives and degree of consistency within the stories around common themes and key events, recall does not appear to have been a problem. In fact, all participants were very keen and engaged with the interviews and were committed to sharing their views.

Bryman (2008) outlines examples of where narrative analysis has been applied to interview transcripts, noting that follow-up questions are important in keeping the flow of the discussion, so these were carefully placed at key points in the interviews to retain flow. The important point here is that wherever possible, participants were allowed to talk unimpeded and narrate the issues they felt were important. If the discussion veered in a different direction, a follow-up prompt brought it back to the issue at hand; although in some cases, the participants did this anyway, reflecting their degree of empowerment and the relaxed nature of the interviews despite the weaknesses of using video-conferencing technology. As Bryman (2008) concludes, there are two approaches to the use of narrative analysis: first is the purposeful collection of stories, with the desire to analyse those stories; second, its use as an approach to analyse qualitative data that was not principally designed to capture stories; in our case it is the latter that applied. So, having collected the data, the issue of data analysis arose. The key issues the researchers had to address in the analysis stage are outlined in Table 3.2, which was compiled from Bryman (2008), Charmaz (2003) and Lofland et al. (2006).

Table 3.2 Data-analysis process followed in the analysis of interviews

	Data-analysis process	*Other considerations*
Step 1	• Researchers read the text as a whole and make note at the end • Focus on looking for what is needed to understand what the transcripts are about • Identify the major themes in the narrative to understand what is happening and key events • Group the narrative in the text into categories, perhaps aligned to research questions for other key criteria (e.g. respondent type and organisation type)	• As Charmaz (2003) argues, this stage is about seeking an understanding of: What is going on?, What are people saying/doing?

	Data-analysis process	*Other considerations*

Step 2	• Mark the text (either using paper copies or a software tool like NVivo)
	• Make notes in the margins
	• Develop labels for the codes which the researchers have developed
	• Highlight key words
	• Note any ideas around the analysis
		• In creating codes in qualitative analysis, it is seen as good practice for two researchers to independently complete stages 1 and 2 independently before meeting to agree codes
		• According to Lofland et al. (2006), in developing codes, there are a range of categories to consider that may help in their formulation. These are as follows:
		
		  ▪ Acts
		  ▪ Activities (i.e. the setting and people involved in these)
		  ▪ Meanings (i.e. concepts used or meanings attached to ideas)
		  ▪ Participation (e.g. involvement in the issues being examined)
		  ▪ Relationships between different aspects of the research
		  ▪ Settings (i.e. the context)

Step 3	• Mark the text with the codes to identify key elements in the narrative • Review the codes and text to eliminate repetition, which may be achieved by combining some codes • Think of groupings that may have been left out of the codes	
Step 4	• Begin to relate general ideas from the literature to the narrative to begin the interpretive stage • Identify the significance of the knowledge being created • Look at the interconnections between the codes	• Begin to identify elements in the narrative that could help illustrate the arguments in the write-up

Source: Bryman (2008), Charmaz (2003) and Lofland et al. (2006)

These four stages were followed in the data analysis to collate the relevant themes and sub-themes. The codes developed by each researcher were then compared and standardised, which creates a degree of coherence to the text. However, often multiple themes arose from a section of narrative, and these were best read in their totality multiple times in order to better understand the complexity.

One of the key debates on using material from narratives is how to illustrate key findings and arguments and the extent of verbatim quotations that should be deployed. Bryman (2008: 697) summarised the debate over using quotations, describing them as designed 'to reinforce or illustrate points they are making about the themes they extracted from their data'. Verbatim interview quotations, as examined by Corden and Sainsbury (2006), were used for different purposes, including providing the participants with a voice, or to further evidence an argument as well as to enrich the readers' understanding of a theme. Verbatim quotations comprise several types in our study:

- The occasional use of an *extended quotation* as a self-contained narrative of a theme that many other participants have mentioned, which establishes the historical development, context and outcome of certain actions
- As *an illustrative quotation* of an argument or interpretation of a theme, typically as a short extract and not exceeding 100 or so words, which reinforces the different realities and experiences of a specific issue
- As a very *short but pointed comment* by one or more participants (often under 50 words) that either illustrates a standalone argument or part of a wider argument in combination with other quotations. In this way, we focused attention on why certain actions occurred, or particular viewpoints of a similar or divergent nature.

In each case, the process of selection and the extent of the narrative included meant that only a representative set of quotations were used in view of the limited extent of the 'Focus' book model. In some instances where the narrative on specific themes could be summarised (i.e. what a programme had done to change something), it was presented in a tabulated format to aid understanding of issues of scope, scale and extent of actions in the age-friendly programmes.

Findings

Characteristics of staff responsible for age-friendly initiatives

The first stage in exploring the age-friendly journey in different localities was, to begin with, a very broad scoping question to understand the background of the people responsible for the AFCs and help contextualise the responses and perspectives offered in the interviews. The responses indicate the heterogeneous nature of the participants, which helps us to recognise that a diverse range of factors shape how individuals and groups of people have progressed the age-friendly agenda. These include educational background, training, work environment and culture, and the approach and agenda of the organisation as regards ageing. The majority of participants worked in local authorities (17), whilst six were from charities such as local Age UK offices, and five were from an amalgam of private limited companies, national government agencies, grant-funded bodies and other organisations. The majority of participants were from a public health background, where many of the initiatives were located (seven), whilst others were from social-care backgrounds, were managers of leading charities or had recently been appointed age-friendly officers, and had a range of experience relevant to the initiative. For example, as one participant indicated, *'as I say, it came from that asset-based approach. So, obviously, that was my background, community development'* [P3]. The participants' collective experience of ageing issues was a total of 294.5 years with an average of around 10 years each, with some having upwards of 30 years of work experience in the field. This is vividly illustrated by the following participant:

> So I've started this role since January 2017, but I've worked around the age-friendly programme . . . since pre-2010, probably 2006, so I've been involved in ageing type initiatives and work, age-friendly work since 2006, mainly through things like neighbourhood regeneration, neighbourhood-based kind of working . . . I've had a long association with the programme, so I've kind of worked with the programme . . . then . . . in 2017 actually joined the programme directly . . . as a programme lead. [P5]

This summarises the long-term engagement with the ageing agenda that was replicated in the career history of other participants, and which has the advantage of helping to provide the knowledge base for the age-friendly agenda along two axes: vertically and horizontally. In vertical terms, it does so through a deeper understanding of the issues which ageing poses for human populations, so the phenomenon is appreciated as a specialist subject. Horizontally, the value is in how that knowledge is communicated to other people in the organisations they engage with internally and externally. Here, they can draw upon that subject knowledge to illustrate how their work impacts an older population and where that work can engage, or

already is engaging an age-friendly agenda and, as more than one participant indicated, pose a challenge to

> *ageism and inequality. Because we know . . . ageism exists in all sorts of*
> *forms, either through benign kind of dismissal or kind of active kind of*
> *dismissal you get. I mean, in the world of work and elsewhere it's alive*
> *and well, so the third priority for us is attacking ageism and addressing*
> *that as well, with positive images and positive kind of representation of*
> *older people.* [P5]

The importance of challenging the status quo within organisations and
society was implicit in many of the comments by participants during the
discussions. A commitment to challenging inequality was a theme running
throughout the narratives, which emerged in an unprompted manner and
illustrated the respondents' deep commitment to and professional concern
with working towards the public good.

As Jenkins et al. (2016) acknowledged (citing a study by Willmott et al.
2016), public health moving to local authorities has now created a delicate
balance for its practitioners who must carry on their professional activities,
whilst taking into account the need to achieve political accountability and
the influence of local politics. At the same time, it has also offered opportunities to shape public agendas such as the age-friendly area, with many
explicit and implicit influences from a public health perspective. These
observations are also relevant for other officers outside of the public health
field, reiterating the challenges of managing complexity in local government. This complexity was highlighted by one participant in terms of how
they interpret the AFC model and implement it in their work using the concept of age-friendly neighbourhoods:

> *So it's about the places, the physical environment, the housing, the ser-*
> *vices in those places being age-friendly and meeting your needs . . . so*
> *it's about services being age aware, having an age-friendly lens to what*
> *they do. It's not about creating age-specific services, but often we're*
> *told, well, why do we need to talk about older people because our ser-*
> *vice is universal? But like many universal services . . . you don't meet*
> *the needs of LGBT people, you don't meet the needs of . . . older people*
> *because you're not thinking about how it might be different for them.*
> *They might need the same service, but you might need to communicate*
> *it or offer it or deliver it in a slightly different way, that you will encour-*
> *age those people to access it.* [P5]

The quotation also addresses the arguments and case for adopting an age-friendly lens combined with a whole-neighbourhood approach, so that a positive approach to ageing can be embedded in service delivery in local communities. The quotation also demonstrates some of the positive attributes of an age-friendly paradigm in shifting thinking in public-service delivery. This also recognises the complex issues associated with communities that are not easily reduced to standardised management practices.

Several studies in the field of public administration offer insights into the roles of local government staff and their management tasks that are relevant to the age-friendly agenda. Getha-Taylor and Morse (2013) explore these attributes, arguing that traditional management models (e.g. the bounded hierarchical organisation – see Lewin 1935) need to be moderated due to the collaboration and problem-solving tasks which are required in local government organisations, with their flatter organisational structures and more unbounded hierarchies that allow cross-boundary working. These points are reflected in P5's narrative above, on boundary crossing and influencing thinking, which raises a broader issue around the competencies required in a local government setting. Fisher (2007) characterised the scope of elected government officials' competencies as needing to be policymakers, communicators, facilitators, enablers, negotiators, financiers, overseers, power brokers and decision-makers. This builds upon some of the classic arguments in the leadership literature that Fisher's competencies also apply to many local government managers and staff because of the nature of the work they undertake within a collaborative framework. Perhaps one of the most critical competencies that the management literature has traditionally associated with organisational success is leadership. Bass' (1990) review of the leadership literature identified 12 different definitions of leadership that can be summarised as follows:

1. the focus of group processes;
2. a matter of personality;
3. a matter of inducing compliance;
4. the exercise of influence;
5. limited to discretionary influence;
6. an act or behavior;
7. a form of persuasion;
8. a power relationship;
9. an instrument of goal achievement;
10. an emerging effect of interaction;

11. the initiation of structure; and
12. a combination of elements

Source: Svensson and Wood 2005: 1002–3

Interestingly, Svara (1985) compared the elected-official and local-government-officer roles, observing that a complex relationship existed between the two and that whilst the mission and policymaking were broadly associated with the elected official, the local government manager was concerned with administration and management functions. However, Svara (1985) did note the blurring of the boundaries between these roles. Extending this debate further, Hendriks et al. (2015) highlighted the intersectoral approaches adopted in local government as well as the important role of persuasion (defined as communication to stimulate action) as a key competence of the local government manager. Applying these considerations to the age-friendly initiative, it is also important to recognise the importance of the capacity and capability of organisations in undertaking new projects. Gargan (1981) outlined the interdependencies that exist in managing projects in a public-sector setting, where policy, resources and programme management are important elements in achieving project success. These are complemented by the ability to forge interconnections across council departments to access different budgets to help with capacity building around a cross-cutting theme such as ageing.

In terms of the management of the age-friendly workstream, a range of organisational models of development emerge from the narratives. Some programmes were located within public health teams, who were either leading the initiative or managing an age-friendly officer or team or both; others were led by individuals with a background in public health or a cognate area who were located in other areas (e.g. adult social care, social work or an older-person programme); whilst others were steered by individual age-friendly officers leading the initiative pan-council. An alternative model was being led by a charitable body through to a town councillor (see p. 86). Where a non-governmental organisation external to the council was leading the initiative, it was usually in close collaboration with key individuals in the council in order to help embed the initiative in the locality, as we explore later. However, what also needs to be distinguished here is that where senior staff were leading the initiative (alongside those not holding an age-friendly officer role), they were often combining this with other substantive responsibilities as managers, a point to which we will return. One participant illustrated this in a very transparent manner, thus:

*I think there is that embedded focus on what we need to do to get there,
we've got, you know, an age-friendly strategy, we've got an age-friendly
plan but obviously the last year has been somewhat difficult because of
the pandemic and so in the early phases, certainly for the first 2 or 3
months, I was so busy with the drug and alcohol stuff and getting up to
speed with the knowledge . . . [P6]*

These different models of operating the age-friendly delivery model, shown
in Figure 3.3, illustrate the issues around communication, cross-council
working and challenges in developing the age-friendly journey in management terms. The type of governance needed to oversee the age-friendly
process typically comprised a steering group, normally led by a senior manager within the council or organisation. For example, 11 of the participants
highlighted that they were championing the initiative in their organisation,
which reflected their seniority and role, whilst five were not responsible
for the initiative but for the immediate operational needs of that initiative, aligned to their role. A further four participants were co-leading the
development, often in combination with an elected official who was a cabinet member responsible for overseeing the portfolio in which ageing was
located. In some cases, this was a senior political leader such as a mayor or
former Member of Parliament. This illustrates the arguments put forward
by Hysing (2014), who sets out how to gain access to influential people in
order to shape policy as managers. Here the key skills required, as Hysing
(2014) suggested, are networking, communication skills and an ability to
draw upon external resources (e.g. grants) to help push the age-friendly
agenda forwards and to keep the momentum going.

As the following quotations suggest, the varying responsibilities among
those people managing age-friendly schemes combine a wide range of
skills, backgrounds and competencies, which align with those set out by
Gargan (1981). In the following example, the person was

*overseeing a programme of work that involves asset-based community
development, lead for mental health and wellbeing, age-friendly city
work, anything Covid related at the moment. [P24]*

This was not at all dissimilar to other participants with a broad work portfolio who indicated that they:

*. . . work in policy and strategy and cover the following areas: ageing
well (how council services can support residents to age well), refugee
and migrants (how council services can be more accessible and public*

affairs rights around no recourse to public funds) and workforce diver-sity (how we facilitate and support career progression so that senior levels of leadership are more diverse). [P25]

More specifically, one participant identified many of the features discussed above in terms of the typical tasks which their role involved at an operational level; these comprised

Facilitating, collaborating, bringing partners together to instil change, emails, writing action plans, chairing meetings. Influencing and embedding public health at a neighbourhood level[,] particularly health improvement and tackling health inequalities. [P26]

Within these three quotations, several key themes emerge. Age-friendly work is not necessarily the participant's sole focus and so they have to allocate some of their time to this work as part of a broader portfolio of non-age-friendly work. Instilling a change agenda is a key component of the organisation's age-friendly journey organisation, which reiterates the broader discussion of values and concern about inequality and the community. Above all, several participants highlighted the way in which the age-friendly programme interconnects with many of the other tasks they have to perform.

Jehu et al. (2018) emphasised the negotiating and networking skills of Public Health Officers in their new local authority environment and their importance in change agendas such as ageing. In many cases, this change agenda was articulated in how they made connections to healthy-ageing/ageing-well strategies. The age-friendly agenda, in many cases, was an evolution of this policy work although as we shall discuss later, it also had the potential to duplicate work in cases where other ageing agendas pre-dated and continued to compete with the programme. This policy connection was demonstrated by one participant, who indicated that they had 'recently influenced our health and wellbeing board to have a priority for ageing well, which was agreed in September 2020' [P26].

The key tasks of an age-friendly officer were distinct from the broader-portfolio model of programme development; as one officer observed, their role was far more targeted, seeking to:

Establish and administer an Age-Friendly Alliance that will develop and implement an Age-Friendly Strategy and 3 Year Action Plan. Support and build on an Age-Friendly Older Persons Council (ABC Seniors Network). Building up the Age-Friendly Agenda within Council [and] [r]aise awareness of Age-Friendly through partnerships with

key stakeholders, Age Northern Ireland, and community and voluntary
sector. Consultation and engagement with older people/older people's
groups. Project Monitoring and Evaluation. [P27]

This summarises many of the features which other age-friendly officers outlined. This quotation closely mirrors what Menec (2017: 103, 105) termed
'building coalitions' (which may also be termed partnerships):

> *Coalitions are formed because of the recognition that working together*
> *is a more effective means to promote social change than if individual*
> *groups or organizations were to function in isolation . . . In age-friendly*
> *initiatives, creating coalitions or partnerships among diverse organi-*
> *zations and across sectors has been identified as an important aspect of*
> *becoming more age-friendly (e.g. Garon et al. 2014; Menec et al. 2014;*
> *Neal et al. 2014; Plouffe et al. 2013), as no one organization or sector*
> *can deal with the full range of age-friendly domains on its own . . . For*
> *example, successful coalitions have a shared vision and mission among*
> *members, follow formal governance procedures, encourage strong*
> *leadership, foster active participation and collaboration among mem-*
> *bers, and enable group cohesion.*

Again, this indicates the importance of leadership and power in terms of
influencing a diverse range of internal and external actors.

The experiences of the broader-portfolio and age-friendly-officer models
of development begin to provide insights into the scope and extent of the
work involved in the age-friendly journey within the sponsoring organisation (e.g. planning and engagement), as well as the external perspective
(e.g. community and stakeholder engagement) of the WHO domains. Different experiences emerged where a charity or other organisation was leading the age-friendly initiative as the following extended quotation on the
lived experience of developing the age-friendly journey suggests:

> *in 2017 . . . one of the directors from the local authority was working*
> *with my predecessor. And they decided that they were going to put on*
> *a conference for older people to talk about . . . age-friendly issues. So*
> *I . . . picked it up before the conference happened. And the thing for*
> *us was that, unfortunately older people do tend to fall off the agenda*
> *very easily. If you get a group of people together and talk about, 'What*
> *should we focus on?', at present it would tend to be young people and*
> *mental health, they're very much the in topics. And so we wanted to do*
> *something that would bring together older people and people that work*
> *with them and find out, actually, what do they think age-friendly means*

and what things do they think need to happen. And so we held a confer-
ence in 2017 and that was the start of it all, and the real reason was to
move it up on the agenda . . . I also work a lot within the community.
And so in terms of having the links there, I think it was just felt that that
would be a good arrangement. I mean, in effect, I think it's fair, because
basically I work with a team here and I work with a team at the Coun-
cil. And we're all working towards the same end and it does work. And
why they chose to do it like that, I think it's just because I was there at
the beginning, I was pushing it forward, and so they thought, well, let's
work round what we've got rather than creating something new. [P16]

From this quotation, it can be seen that first a grassroots stimulus to develop
a much stronger emphasis on ageing within a community emerged, which
then developed into the age-friendly initiative. There is a clear political theme
here from a lobbying perspective: the need to move ageing higher up the
agenda, as other hot topics were attracting greater attention from a national
and local perspective. This example also illustrates how the programme was
built around existing relationships and projects in a partnership model. The
quotation also raises two pertinent question – how typical were these experiences of developing the age-friendly programme in localities, and were
there specific factors promoting the development of the programme?

How did the age-friendly idea come about in each locality?

Table 3.1 outlines the timeline for each locality starting the age-friendly
journey. As seen in Chapter 2 and as noted by McGarry (2019), the antecedents of age-friendly work can be found in ageing projects and strategies
for some localities that pre-dated the age-friendly initiative. These provided
the groundwork for becoming an AFC in some cases, whilst in others, the
connection was not as clear-cut. The narratives illustrate that the initial stimulus to pursue the age-friendly journey appears to have emerged from four
potential sources, summarised in Figure 3.4 (see p. 86). In a considerable
number of the transcripts, remaining connected with the person leading the
age-friendly initiative (whether they were a politician or senior colleague)
was deemed important to keep the project moving forwards, a point also
observed by Svara (1985) and Hysing (2014). The importance of political
influence, power and a champion to progress the project is demonstrated in
the following narrative of how one locality became age-friendly:

the work on becoming an age-friendly XXXX was first raised by the
group of organisations . . . [which] were some of our key partner

organisations in terms of delivery of services to older people, and they came and did a deputation to Council Assembly where they asked the Council to become an age-friendly city, and then it went, and this was just before the election in 2014, and it was adopted as part of the Labour Party manifesto . . . I know different Local Authorities have different processes but largely what happens in terms of developing the Council plan in XXXXX is that lots of the Council plan targets are derived from the manifesto of the successful party, so it then became a Council plan target, and it was really interesting about the way in which it developed internally in terms of responsibility [by] xxxx . . . who had worked in older person's services within adult social care, kind of for years and years and years, one of the things that we were really clear about was that we wanted this to be about how people aged not just focused on the services for older people which we felt was far too narrow a concept, so in fact I think the original Cabinet paper that started the process off and sort of agreed that we would approach the World Health Organization for this status, was actually written by a person in housing strategy you know, not that this was kind of linked to her but it was about somebody who had you know, those particular strengths to develop and kind of pull this together, and then they got me onboard around [. . .] well we know that what we all need to do in order to develop a strategy and to kind of start the journey is we will actually need kind of the skills and talents around communities because we'll need to talk to people and we will need to continue this as a process where there's all the key organisations that are supporting older people as well as others within the community, are kind of brought on board and carried forward, so that was very much our thinking, and I think you know, one of the things that we did really, really well is it was a collaborative process in terms of kind of making the decision about becoming age-friendly, and in terms of identifying in that first report that we did about what it was that we needed to change in order to become age-friendly. [P14]

This lengthy reflective quotation outlines how the age-friendly concept was developed in one locality as a basis from which to ascertain whether this experience, or components of it, was replicated elsewhere, or whether other localities had different age-friendly trajectories that were shaped by different influences or influencers. In this quotation, several key strands emerge from the historical narrative as themes around the age-friendly journey:

- First is the importance of an advocate, which in this instance was a coalition of groups with an interest in ageing that placed it on a political party's agenda

- Second, there was a receptive audience to the idea, which was then endorsed by the council planning process to initiate the project
- Third, someone with considerable experience in ageing championed the idea within the council and the WHO application was made to align this with the ambition to become an AFC
- Fourth, someone with strategic experience was co-opted in order to bring a community focus
- Fifth, a wide range of actors were involved in the development process from idea to implementation
- Sixth, a review was undertaken to outline the actions needed to become an AFC from an operational perspective, including the baseline study and data collection
- Lastly, the entire process of age-friendly development was undertaken collaboratively

A more detailed assessment of the narratives suggests that there is a degree of consistency with some of these findings, emphasising the interconnected nature of how the programme evolved. From the narratives, several ways in which the programmes evolved can be identified: emanating from a prior decision in the organisation that pre-dated the participant's arrival; a novel idea or innovation with organisational appeal; pursuing a strategic direction for the locality; a potential solution to the ageing issue in the locality; a political dimension with a champion; a response to a national strategy (where these existed); the availability of national funding to support the journey; or a degree of serendipity, where senior staff in the organisation saw the value of this approach to council work and the community. We shall now explore these in the words of the participants to reconstruct the key factors associated with a locality embarking on the age-friendly journey.

In some of the organisations managing the programme, the decision to become an age-friendly locality pre-dated the appointment of some the participants and it became a delegated responsibility for someone else to implement. This is illustrated by a very typical response which explained how a

> . . . *cabinet member for adult social care, he thought it would be a good idea. So hence it's been delegated down to staff.* [P1]

Where the champion was external to the council, sometimes the combination of different interests resulted in a decision, but the lead officer then left the organisation. This then led to a vacuum of leadership as indicated in the following case, where

there was a champion external to the Council, who was really inter-
ested in this area of work, who developed it with a member, an officer
within the Council . . . And they put a lot of energy into it and got things
started and put a lot of time and energy and dedication into it within
the Council. It would be fair to say that that Council officer left the
organisation and the next person who picked it up didn't have the same
enthusiasm for the topic . . . they then left the organisation and I've
picked it up and tried to reignite some of that enthusiasm, you know,
and some dedicated time to the topic. [P8]

Similar stories about how interest was sparked in this theme are evident in
the following two quotations. In the case of a charitable organisation leading the initiative,

it actually started, for us, in 2017 and one of the directors from the
local authority was working with my predecessor. And they decided
that they were going to put on a conference for older people to talk
about sort of age-friendly issues. So I sort of picked it up before the
conference happened. [P16]

Whilst in a local authority setting:

it was always an aspiration as a Council to be age-friendly since
I started. We do have a cabinet member who has got lead responsibil-
ity for adult social care in public health, so the present councillor is
particularly interested in older people, she's a social worker for back-
ground and has got a particular interest in . . . age-friendly, and actually
chairs one of our age-friendly groups, and I think when I first started
we had as an Authority looked at becoming an age-friendly XXXX but
never had really taken it forward, but it was our health and well-being
board were very keen for us to become . . . age-friendly, to join the
WHO age-friendly community [. . .] we report back to the health and
well-being board which is also chaired by the . . . leader of the Council
and obviously has external partners, so I think it's both internally and
externally driven and I'd say officer driven as well in terms of there's a
great commitment within the Local Authority and the external partners
to really drive this agenda forward. [P7]

In the last two quotations, it is evident that different trajectories exist in
terms of the evolution of the programme. The charitable organisation
convened a conference with the local authority to develop a grassroots
approach to scope out the issues. In contrast, in the second quotation, a

political decision emerged, as the council had decided to pursue the direction but never progressed it. In this case, interest was reignited by a health and well-being board that has since helped rekindle interest and join up the locality agendas, whilst the council have taken ownership of the initiative's development.

In some instances, this was part of recognising the creativity associated with a novel idea or innovation that had organisational appeal and was potentially part of a new way of thinking promoted by a cabinet member. Yet as the following quotation suggests, adopting an innovative idea and then asking a council to implement it requires both buy-in and resources to embed the new approach:

> *I think there was one Councillor in XXXX who had seen another Council area undertaking this and thought it would be a good idea for the Council to get you know, to start the age-friendly process so I think there was one Councillor and then once I was in post I did get the age-friendly champions within both Council areas to help champion the age-friendly project you know, but I think like anything . . . that's new it's quite hard to get buy-in and that's how I find it, it's trying to get people to help drive it within Council so it's been a difficult journey in regard to that.* [P18]

Finding a convincing argument to illustrate the perceived benefits of developing an age-friendly approach as a strategic direction for managing ageing appears to have been a success factor in some localities. In the following quotation, the participants draw together the different strands of these arguments by interconnecting an age-friendly programme with seeking a solution to the problems of ageing, whilst illustrating that enhancements for one group will also benefit others in the community, a theme that resurfaced several times in the narratives:

> *The reason for doing this was to explore a range of ways of managing the demands presented by the city's ageing population. Like many cities, XXXX is expecting its population to become increasingly aged, with residents aged over 60 projected to increase from 24% in 2012 to 31.2% in 2037. Our desire to be an age-friendly city was driven by the acknowledgement of improving things for older people should also benefit people of all ages – we want XXXX to be inclusive of all people, including children and young people and other protected characteristics, such as BAME and disability.* [P25]

The notion of seeking a potential solution to the ageing issue in the locality emerged again in the following comments:

> *our former MP . . . was very, very acutely aware of the problems that older people in the area, and particularly xxxx would face, and will be facing in the light of local authority cuts, and a particular situation in which Age UK xxxx changing its method of delivery for services for older people in the town.* [P2]

This quotation also highlights a political dimension very similar to that of the extended narrative on p. 79, with the added concern about how to offset potential services to older people in a period of austerity. Yet the political dimension within organisations also emerged, where competing ageing agendas and potential fiefdoms existed due to the council signing up to other ageing agendas, as the following quotation demonstrates:

> *when we signed up to The Dublin Declaration in 2011, there had just been local elections, and there was a councillor on the cabinet who had been given sort of ageing within her portfolio, she had just come into post . . . And she came to the Dublin conference and she took a very proactive lead as . . . political leadership around age-friendly, so that's how she championed that commitment from the city. And it had, you know, sort of alongside her it had some senior officer input as well, as well as you know, I continued to do what I would call the more sort of day-to-day stuff, you know, secretariat for the . . . partnership group when we committed to the WHO we set up a new group, which included many of the same partners of course, but you know, we did make a demarcation, we had this very strong political leadership from a politician who was very committed. Now that lasted for, I think she was on the cabinet for about three years . . . And then when they had the next reshuffle of the City Council cabinet, she was not, that particular individual was not elected to the cabinet, and the age-friendly portfolio was sort of morphed [. . .] into what was the Healthy Cities portfolio . . . And we were a part of that, and we continued to have links to that. So for us, and you know, and it isn't resolved in the WHO, it just is not helpful really, you've got the European Healthy Cities group, which has this healthy ageing taskforce, which is using, to some extent interpreting . . . the age-friendly cities framework but doing it within the Healthy Cities movement, and then you have the global, you know, age-friendly network led from a different part of the WHO.* [P9]

In Northern Ireland and Wales, a national commitment to become age-friendly meant that the evolution of the initiative was a top-down innovation in which localities developed the advances of previous ageing work. In the case of Wales, the initiative covered 22 local authority areas and 11 in Northern Ireland. One participant explained how the process of becoming age-friendly worked in the devolved government areas. Their region was the

> *first council area to become members of the World Health Organisation Age-Friendly Communities Network and . . . our Active Ageing strategy which is central government . . . was released and it very much has its mantra of XXXX becoming age-friendly. There's a network and we're serviced by the Department of Communities and . . . our arm of Age UK and also the Public Health Agency, which have been very involved. The Public Health Agency have been very proactive, they're sort of like a commissioning body for the health service. So they actually have funded a number of age-friendly coordinator posts.* [P15]

As this quotation indicates, the availability of funding aligned to a national strategy was a key stimulus to success, a feature other participants also mentioned. Where a charity was leading the programme, funding streams were also crucial in pump-priming the age-friendly journey, as shown in the following example:

> *When I started in post in 2013 my role was around dementia-friendly communities, and dementia-friendly and age-friendly sit, link incredibly well, you know, actually if you're dementia-friendly you are age-friendly, and if you're age-friendly you are quite dementia-friendly as well. So at the point of time when the Ageing Better money, which is the lottery fund that had supported this work . . . was out . . . [and] the bids were open, we applied, and Age UK were the lead and there were a number of different projects that sat under that Ageing Better funding, and one of them that we bid for was for an age-friendly project. So we've worked on this for, this is our seventh year now.* [P22]

From the viewpoint of the binary perspective through which management theory examines how new ideas are implemented in organisations, it is assumed that organisational performance is directly related to objective measures of management. Yet as Svensson and Wood (2005) observed, the role of serendipity is also significant. Their analysis of serendipity identifies different definitions that reveal a variety of elements to the concept and its unpredictable role in organisational effectiveness – it may comprise luck, an unexpected discovery, or a chance meeting that creates an opportunity. Cunha et al.'s (2010) philosophical review of the concept also noted the notion of impedance, which may inhibit this process in organisations where vested interests or power dynamics limit its impact. Even so, at least one participant explicitly stated that serendipity had been a factor: '*when I retired here . . . I was persuaded to go on the XXXX Council, that was my first priority to make the XXXX Council age-friendly, which is where we're up to*' [P12]. What is not evident from this brief quotation is that the participant had been heavily involved in steering the development of one of the most successful programmes, so although serendipity had a role to play, they brought a substantial body of experience and knowledge to the role. Implicit in some of the narratives was a decision to embark on the age-friendly journey resulting from a chance meetings or discussion that had ignited the idea, and so such experiences should not be underestimated.

The interconnections between the themes are evident from reading any of the transcripts, as arbitrarily separating the narratives into themes does not always do justice to the complexity within the text, as this quotation from a participant leading a programme from within a charity highlights:

Well there's always been a massive support for age-friendly, because the [locality] have a high ageing demographic, so we have a population of X, and . . . 50% of those are over the age of 50, and 24.7% over the age of 65. I think what would be fair to say is the age-friendly initiative, they [the Council] have become more on board with, as we've developed it, so we, . . . have had various Council departments represented on our age-friendly steering group, and our age-friendly steering group is made up of private-public and voluntary sector organisations, we have about 32 organisations on that steering group, and they are the real driving force of age-friendly, and as I say those Council departments that are on there, so from the start we had, at the time the . . . Fire Service, library service, Trading Standards, and a representative from public health was on there where they weren't necessarily part of the Council at that time, so it's all changed in the seven years, but that's developed, and as we've kind of created those partnerships, developed partnership projects, have had impact, and have . . . made . . . cultural change . . . so the Council has become more on board. And I would say at the beginning of our sixth year we have, I've been seconded to XXXX Council to look at how we embed the age-friendly work, within the . . . Council, and that we're about to do for the seventh year. [P22]

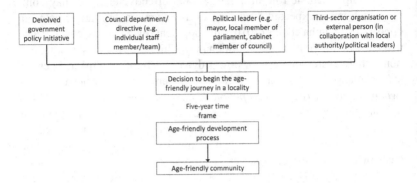

Figure 3.3 Model of age-friendly programme initiation and leadership

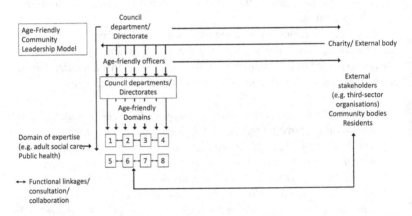

Figure 3.4 Model of age-friendly programme development

In this instance, the trajectory towards becoming age-friendly evolved from associated strands of funded work, initially on dementia and then the age-friendly programme.

So what do the interviews tell us about the leadership of the age-friendly initiative in terms of success? Returning to Bass' (1990) original 12 categories of leadership, each of the different definitions are discernible in the narratives, grouped around words such as 'collaboration', 'partnership working', 'co-production' and similar terms that capture how leadership has helped move the programme forwards to gain momentum. The types of leadership outlined by Bass (1990) are visible in the narratives either explicitly or implicitly, with different approaches evident in how AF programmes are led and managed. Among the attributes that emerged in the narratives were the role of group processes, different personalities in leading the programme, influencing, persuasion, power relationships and the creation of structures. Yet one should not underestimate the difficulties identified by Woo and Choi (2022), who observed that though there may be considerable enthusiasm when initiating the idea of becoming an AFC, it is more challenging for age-friendly officers to get others to buy in to the project later, and there is a need to galvanise support from 'champions' within the organisation to establish momentum and acceptance and implementation of the age-friendly process in their work. It also highlights the challenges of working on age-friendly issues in gaining resources and how leadership can help negotiate some of these challenges.

Working challenges

Participants were asked to consider the types of challenges they faced in dealing with older people; these have also been discussed at length in the academic literature by Menec and Brown (2018) and are summarised in Table 2.3. A number of the barriers identified by Menec and Brown were also identified by the participants: a change in policy direction, turnover in leadership, lack of volunteers/volunteer burnout, lack of skills, the conflict between groups, competing interests, lack of common objectives, lack of funding and a lack of common approach/criteria. A number of these barriers were also observed in this study, but a wider range of challenges emerged that reflect the nuances of the way different localities have approached the development of AFCs (as highlighted earlier in Figure 3.2). In the UK setting, we framed the discussion in terms of challenges in order to elicit responses that did not begin the discussion in a negative way by using a term like 'problem', 'barrier' or another phrase that might be interpreted negatively. The word 'challenges' inferred that these issues may be overcome with solutions, as opposed to being barriers that might prevent the initiative from developing any further.

From the UK perspective, a range of themes emerge around the following areas, although we need to stress these are not necessarily mutually exclusive as they are interconnected. First, *engagement and communication with older people* and the *effect of Covid* were identified; these also seemed to be compounded by *geographical variations in inequality and engagement*. This illustrates the interconnected nature of these challenges, which were part of a web of broader societal issues associated with ageing in a locality. These issues had several aspects, including *digital exclusion and micro engagement issues* – who were the right people to involve? General concerns around engagement were raised, as illustrated in the following two quotations identifying the key challenges:

> *Trying to engage older people.* [P24]
>   *Challenges are broad ranging from ensuring inclusive approaches to meeting local people's needs, heightened by the Covid-19 pandemic.* [P26]

The layers of complexity begin to emerge when we recognise that the age-friendly initiative is about co-producing services and environments with older people: in the words of one respondent, '*it's just very challenging to do that, you know, in the full co-productive way that we would want to do that*' [P8]. The effect of Covid is referred to throughout the transcripts, as the interviews were undertaken amid a lockdown which brought about significant changes to the operation of age-friendly activity, as the following quotation illustrates:

> *Pre-Covid. I suppose a big lot of things that we would have done . . . loads of events. Tea dances are my speciality, obviously I'm doing virtual tea dances right now. But we also have discos . . . and different things and I suppose it's getting that engagement and I suppose it's people not considering themselves older, wanting to go to an older people's events and things and we have a really good structure of older people's networks in XXXX which we're a tiny bit concerned how it will survive Covid.* [P15]

When one then considers the social profile of many communities that have an age-friendly programme, the nuances of the locality in terms of deprivation and the social geography of the area pose micro-level issues around inequality as this quotation from a charitable body suggests:

> *this is an area . . . of high social deprivation. It's also an area that, a lot of commissioning is done at a very local level, and that's really important because the different areas are so different to each other. So your life expectancy if you live on the XXXX side of XXXX is a lot lower than your life expectancy is if you live in the XXXX side, which is the more affluent, rural side of it.* [P16]

The gap in life expectancy for men within the locality is seven years between the most affluent and most deprived areas; the region is in the upper quartile of the most deprived local authorities in England, based on the government's Index of Multiple Deprivation. In contrast, the following quotation from a region with a large rural hinterland identified different types of challenges, associated with inaccessibility and poor digital connectivity:

> *Our infrastructure wouldn't be fabulous, we have problems with communication and broadband . . . into the rural areas . . . our district is basically two major towns, seven larger towns and then the rest are villages.* [P15]

In a more urban locality, this was also reframed in terms of the affordability of internet access; here, the problem was caused by poverty and lack of knowledge of how to use the internet. The major challenges were a

> *lack of funding to be able to commission good work that is taking place in the voluntary and community sector, stretched resources to be able to deliver projects that would be of benefit to residents such as more intense digital inclusion support and lack of time and skills to be able to proactively reach marginalised groups of older residents.* [P25]

Interestingly another district made up of a large city, smaller towns and a rural hinterland identified the challenges as being similar:

> *. . . the challenges I think would be really communication and even just physically getting to some of the groups or the older people . . . . I don't think, to be honest I don't think there's a massive difference between rural and urban . . . it's the same things, transport, housing, communications, broadband . . . we're a small population we are harder to reach actually, but it is very very similar across the district, I think.* [P15].

In the following quotation, a participant highlighted the philosophical approach they had adopted and were trying to embed as a world view on ageing, rooted in a social approach that was underpinned by ageing well, and taking account of people's needs and the inherent inequalities in society:

> *our programme is very much based on that social approach . . . we sit in Public Health and it's good in terms of social approach . . . we're not taking a biomedical approach, we're not looking directly at care or frailty or falls . . . other people do that, and our role is to say, how does that fit in to improving, or how does that support people to age well?*

So it's not about, you've had a fall, how do we stop you having one again, it's actually how do you age well, to try and not have a fall or to make that happen far later in your life . . . So that's kind of where we're coming from . . . a lot of the challenge for us then is that, how we get other people, other organisations or directorates within the Council, to take an approach that sees the world like that? So how does Health and Social Care approach ageing in an ageing-well perspective, rather than we provide health services to people? So that's the challenge for our programme, really, is how do we get people to adopt that approach, to develop that thinking, that understanding around the population and the inequalities and the needs of that population, and to do things in a way that is different, that includes the voice of older people and is less about just delivering services. [P5]

Juxtaposed with that quotation was a recognition that the public sector since 2011 has experienced substantial cuts to funding, as illustrated earlier in this chapter and discussed in many domains (e.g. Inman 2021), and that the urban bias (Centre for Cities 2019) has created a more divided society evidenced with an increase in homelessness, rough sleeping and health inequalities (Johns 2020). Therefore, financial constraints remained a key theme which participants mentioned throughout the discussions as a strong subtext in many of their narratives, where they referred to government cuts to core funding for local authorities. But the austerity subtext also co-exists alongside the wider funding problems for charitable bodies, which Clifford (2016) observed during the period of austerity, noting that local government funding of their work also declined and a degree of hollowing out has also impacted their work. This also had a geographical effect that had a greater impact on the more deprived localities in terms of social welfare provision and well-being related to service delivery. Many of the points raised by Clifford (2016) are demonstrated in the following quotation from a charitable organisation leading the programme of age-friendly work:

we're a small local charity, and this is a project of the charity, and we don't actually get any specific funding for the work that we do, we raise bits and pieces here and there, we are commissioned to provide advocacy for older people, so we think of it as collective advocacy really, but there's always a challenge of funding, and keeping things going in that way. I think that what I've found when I came into the organisation was that some of the way we spoke about things was negative, and often quite combative, and not very constructive. And so I've tried to . . . reframe things a little bit, so that we can concentrate a bit more on solutions rather than being antagonistic towards the Council for example. [P4]

From another perspective, a local authority highlighted the scale of recent cuts to funding and its significance to the scope of what could realistically be achieved:

> *there's challenges around buy-in, there's challenges around, I suppose XXXX, as a City Council, we've been hit significantly by austerity. So we've lost something like 64% of the budget in the last ten years, so the workforce is significantly diminished from what it was. So the consequence of that means there are both financial pressures on every officer in the Council and day-to-day additional work pressures because we are now doing the work of what, you know, ten years ago what was the work of one officer, you know, you're now probably doing the work of two or three. And you're trying to do it the best you can, but sometimes, you know, there are only so many hours in the day. So as a result it's, one of the challenges is for people to recognise it as a priority, ageing, the concept, the impact of ageing, the promoting of healthy ageing. So I think the concepts are very much bought into and accepted. But in terms of, well, what do we do about it, it's a lot more challenging when you've got no money, to do something about it.* [P8]

Given the funding issues raised by Clifford (2016), the Covid pandemic had a detrimental impact on the well-being of an ageing population not only in terms of the lockdown but also in the messaging around and treatment of older people by the media. These messages had unintended consequences as the perception of risk contributed to greater levels of social isolation for older age groups, as well as ageist stereotypes of older people (Harper 2020), as the following quotation suggests:

> *Coming out of Covid, the first wave, the board were really unhappy. They could see the way older people were treated in the media in the first lockdown, that kind of herd immunity, frail and vulnerable, locked away, you know, they've said, look, older people and the way we're treated and represented has gone back twenty years in the space of months . . . And they met with our Chief Exec and our leader of the Council to discuss that, about that fact that they felt just dismissed and marginalised. And that led to us preparing a scrutiny paper for our Communities Inequalities scrutiny, political leadership group, and that's been adopted now . . .* [P5]

Among the other significant challenges noted both before and during Covid were those related to communication at two levels: with older people and also within the organisation leading the programme. The internal communication is demonstrated in the following quotation, illustrating the respondents' approach and how they have sought to embed that across their organisation and with partners:

> *we take a social approach to ageing . . . we sit in Public Health . . . it's actually how do you age well, to try and not have a fall or to make that happen far later in your life, you know . . . a lot of the challenge for us then is that, how we get other people, other organisations or directorates within the Council, to take an approach that sees the world like that? So how does Health and Social Care approach ageing in an ageing-well perspective, rather than we provide health services to people? So that's the challenge for our programme, really, is how do we get people to adopt that approach, to develop that thinking . . . to do things in a way that is different, that includes the voice of older people.* [P5]

This approach also has a salience when the political dimension is examined. One participant illustrated why the age-friendly agenda remained so important, given deficits in other government agencies such as Public Health England:

> *Public Health England has nothing in its plan 2020–24 . . . So, public health teams generally speaking, and Directors of Public Health are going to do stuff that kind of aligns with that plan, generally speaking. The NHS has a very limited Ageing Well programme, I've just been looking at it just before we spoke actually, because there's some money hanging around it . . . There's very little in the NHS plan around actually ageing. Public local authority, social care services are struggling . . . I mean, it's all of the above really. How do you cut through then with a story of ageing . . . it's about how do you create a narrative which is realistic and meaningful and mobilises system leaders across a wide range of public and other services, and that's really what my job is.* [P13]

A detailed reading of Public Health England's (PHE) (2019) strategy reveals that it has no mention of ageing in it, but it adopts a parallel agenda to the age-friendly model, which is based on a geographical approach to designing healthier places (to reduce inequalities and improve access to green spaces and leisure opportunities, public services and community facilities). Herein lies a significant political challenge, as in a climate of austerity it is unlikely that two competing agendas will be supported. The PHE approach has also permeated the design of the National Health Service Healthy New Towns programmes as a public health framework. Yet it does not prioritise specific groups, like older people in certain regions. Personal political gratification was also seen as a challenge for some programmes because of the churn in elected officials and cabinet leadership in local government, with the political championing of the AFC often based on serendipity (and political opportunism) whereby someone had specific motives for championing the idea, as illustrated by the following quotation:

> *I think if I'm honest, the politician involved, she was a newly elected councillor, and she was new on the cabinet, and I think what she hoped, and this is my interpretation, was that by championing this agenda it would be a way of her . . . making her mark as a politician.* [P9]

One important consequence of such serendipity is a problem with the continuity of enthusiasm and support for a new idea like an AFC, as will be seen in the following discussion.

Innovation as a work challenge

Menec et al. (2017) argued that being able to influence and then build a coalition of interested parties is a key element of successful models of AFC implementation, and that all parties need to be receptive to innovation and new ideas, a theme highlighted earlier by Participant 18. Innovation as a process has the potential to invoke change; it reflects the culture of the organisation and its openness to absorb new ideas (its absorptive capacity; see Howaldt et al. 2016; Murray et al. 2011). As Hartley (2005: 28) suggested, in public-sector innovation sharing good practices and 'innovations in public and user participation in service design and delivery' is an important part of the innovation process; it appears to be better incorporated where more networked models of governance give more power to policy-makers, and co-production with service users can help drive innovation. In the case of the age-friendly initiative, it is a process-related innovation that seeks to change the way ageing is perceived and incorporated and how services and infrastructure are delivered to that group. Murray et al. (2011), in examining innovation in the public sector, found a series of key factors that determined the absorptive capacity to be an innovative organisation: the level of in-house prior knowledge of the issue; the capacity for informal transfer of both tacit (i.e. people's skills, knowledge and experience, which is not codified and written down) and formal knowledge; the motivation of the people driving the innovation and the intensity of effort expended; and the importance of gatekeepers, as originally argued by Cohen and Levinthal (1990). In terms of that energy and enthusiasm, a charity leading an age-friendly programme summarised its importance succinctly:

> *But it's only where you've got these innovative approaches where someone will go along and champion it, it wouldn't necessarily do it voluntarily without that sort of initial impetus.* [P4]

Gatekeepers can have negative roles in terms of limiting access to specific resources or controlling work practices, but equally, in the case of the age-friendly initiative, can also be harnessed to unlock and undertake boundary-spanning roles where they connect up with other gatekeepers to make things happen, as influencers and drivers of change (i.e. change agents). The positive role of a gatekeeper is illustrated in the case of one locality:

> *We are XXXX Healthy Ageing Strategic Partnership which is our, like, steering group, and unfortunately it was called that before we entered the age-friendly domain . . . and [with] the chair of that we've been really, really lucky. The chair for the last eight years . . . is the Commissioning Lead for the health board . . . He is really . . . he's just amazing and he has got a real broad knowledge and he's involved in so many things, like he's often telling us what's happening in the council because he's at a different level with meetings that we're not and things.* [P15]

Murray et al. (2011) also demonstrate that the gatekeeping role may be held by one person or dispersed across several actors, making the diffusion of innovations a challenging process. Many of the positive and negative aspects of these roles have already been highlighted in the quotations in the previous section; from a strategic perspective, this means that 'Process innovations affect management and organization. They change relationships amongst organizational members and affect rules, roles, procedures and structures, communication and exchange among organizational members' (Walker 2006: 314). All of this needs to be recognised before embarking on an innovation journey. There is also a broader overarching theme that emerges here and that impacts innovation, and that is the political environment within organisations: although gatekeepers may endorse an idea, staff who adopt more laggard behaviour can stifle the innovative process.

The different strands of the experiences from the narratives in the previous section also demonstrate that innovation is a more complex process in a public sector setting than is often acknowledged:

> *Local government organizations must fulfil a dual role in relation to innovation. They must be both generators of innovation – developing new ways to deliver effective services to their constituents – and also implementers of innovation – adopting and diffusing new and effective services developed, for example, by central governments.* (Cropley 2016: 43)

Having established the context of the age-friendly journey in different localities and some of the broad issues associated with developing the initiative, participants were asked about their perception of ageing as a term and how they thought this may have shaped their approach to developing the age-friendly agenda in light of the discussion above on innovation.

Perception of ageing as a construct

Bearing in mind Murray et al.'s (2011) factors affecting the success of innovation, we asked participants about their perception of ageing to understand their level of in-house knowledge, specifically their perspective on ageing as a phenomenon and what it meant to them. This is because it may well have shaped their actions and approach towards developing and implementing age-friendly strategies and actions, particularly the focus within those approaches. This was also an attempt to try and capture the different lenses through which people viewed ageing, based on their professional backgrounds and experience of ageing-related work. Furthermore, this approach may, like the innovation model which Murray introduced, help us to understand whether ageing was seen dynamically with age-friendly developments as a form of innovation (i.e. a process change). Given the lack of clarity and consensus on how different disciplines and subjects approach the concept of ageing, a great diversity of views was expected; we grouped these into sub-themes. To place this discussion in context, the following broad generalisations from the academic literature on ageing are worth summarising, as they demonstrate how the diversity of responses recorded by participants reflects the multiple ways in which the term 'ageing' is constructed by different people:

- General increases in life expectancy have put into question all the chronologically determined criteria that have been used to define when old age begins;

- Old age is biologically inevitable, but how it is defined varies according to how different societies socially construct and perceive it;
- No two human beings are the same, so what may well apply to one person as a categorisation may not apply to another. Ageing is affected by several factors including genetics, career, lifestyle and attitudes;
- Chronologically determined ideologies of age need to be replaced with more flexible and fluid approaches;
- Swift and Steeden (2020), based on the European Social Survey, pointed to significant variations by country on the calendar age definition of old age, with an average of 61 years accepted as the point at which old age begins.

Source: After Page and Connell (2022)

With these generalisations in mind, the themes arising from the discussion of the perception of ageing can be grouped into three distinct areas (although some of the narratives do combine multiple categories within them):

1. Descriptions of ageing and depiction of this using words and tags that comprise different ideas on age as a number; depicting age as a numerical category in an objective way; and lastly, emotive and very subjective evaluations. These emotive and subjective evaluations tend to portray ageing in a relatively negative way.

For example, the idea of age as a number is demonstrated in the following quotations:

So, for me anything past 40 you start to see slight changes and I suppose those escalate as you go along after that, yeah. And it's probably different for everyone, I suppose, different levels and different speeds. [P7]

We kind of class older people as 65 plus, so our services that we commission for older people are 65 plus. But, actually, you know, there's people who are 80 who won't need those services, and there's actually people who are 55 who will. So, broadly speaking, you might say that, you know, the median is 65. [P1]

We, sort of, have this imaginary number in our heads as to what ageing is. And then we see this frail old person and then our language changes to that frail older person. I mean, you know in this modern world, people in their sixties and seventies . . . I mean, I'm in my sixties. We're still working, we're still very active. We're not the same as the people in the 60s, twenty years ago. So, actually, we've got 100-year-olds learning how to use technology for the first time. [P3]

Whereas references to numbers and negative connotations of ageing are expressed by the following participants:

we've looked about how we describe it as an age, ageing well, so you could be you know, age for me is a number, you could be well at 40, you could be well at 90, so I think it's that challenging the number bit you know, oh you're an older person because you're x, what is an older person, so I think it is about how you describe it for, yeah, many people, so elderly, frailty, all these negative connotations we've tried very hard to challenge. [P7]

There are still quite negative connotations of ageing, from your appearance to your health. [P8]

2. Changing perceptions and awareness of multiple viewpoints that portray ageing as a positive attribute and align with the life-course approach, as outlined by Harper (2006) and Quadango (2007), and which are commonly used by public health professionals. In many respects, this approach views ageing as a process occurring through time but which is also unique to the individual and which is shaped by events in that individual's life, as illustrated by the following comments from participants:

I perceive ageing to be a process that is unique to the person but essentially a process of growing older. [P25]

I believe ageing well is a better concept than calling people old, ageing comes to all of us we can embrace it or not – we need to focus on ageing well throughout life so we can live well to a healthy old age. [P26]

We start looking, in terms of Public Health and the ageing-well bit of the life course, we look at 50 plus. [P5]

Before you actually start looking into ageing you have a very negative perception, because I think the media is always very . . . I mean, even if you take the road signs, bent over two people over a stick, and I think when you actually, with the work we do and you see how many opportunities there are out there through ageing, and I think nowadays we're all so much more aware of the health implications and trying to keep ourselves, our bodies and our minds active and healthy. [P20]

3. Ageing as a life stage that needs support, services and infrastructure to be in place to help support ageing well; this reflects a very applied practitioner focus in terms of the life stage approach and how it can

be translated across to meet older people's needs, as the following quotations suggest:

Growing older healthily and actively, engaged and supported. [P24]

I would see ageing as the progression from the beginning of the life cycle to end of the life cycle . . . so each stage of . . . ageing requires different things to be available to us to give us a quality of life . . . it's just the life cycle. [P11]

I think my perception [. . . of] working on ageing, . . . is[,] what do we need to do to enable as many people as possible to age well, so it's not in that sense for me just about older people, it is about more of a life-course approach. [P9]

The term 'ageing' is just about that sort of life cycle and . . . The process I suppose of physically, mentally and getting older. [P15]

In terms of ageing, it's about the life course, it's not just about any age group. [P16]

I think that's like a stereotype and like a quite an ageist attitude towards older people where we're all ageing, but it's a case of how we're structuring our services around our ageing population and I think the penny hasn't dropped yet in terms of people's you know, attitudes towards older people. From my experience it's slightly ageist attitudes that still exist and stereotyping that exists so you're trying to almost change perception of people as they grow older and starting to try to change a culture of how we're thinking of ageing so, but yes I would think of ageing as a population approach. [P18]

Age-friendly is not a programme about services for older people, it is about supporting everybody to age well and understand the requirements and you know, involving people in the design of things to suit that throughout different courses of life stage. [P19]

I suppose it's just the natural passage of time that affects all of us and therefore that's why I feel it should be a universally accepted concept in terms of people will get older but it's about ensuring then that they're able to do so with dignity, that they're able to have local amenities . . . but ultimately a lot of amenities that people, you know, have paid into the system all their lives, when they get older they're just not there because the social infrastructure has disappeared unfortunately, so the result is that deprived communities have seen probably this effect more because they probably had less of stuff to start with and they've seen it withdrawn whereas more affluent communities, I notice, are able to still enjoy those benefits because they have better access to things like green space, they have better access to[.] [P6]

These perceptions of ageing also have salience with a theme that emerged in some of the narratives, namely the importance of political economy as an explanation of why an age-friendly paradigm has developed so much significance.

Political economy and the development of age-friendly communities

Drawing together many of the strands from the narratives on how the AFC programme has developed, several theoretical debates emerge that can be best described as fitting into the field of political economy. Political economy as a mode of analysis is not new in ageing research (Walker 1981; Walker and Foster 2014) or in research on local government (Dollery and Wallis 2001); its focus is broadly defined as how political forces shape organisations' policies, and how political institutions, the political environment and economic system interact to create outcomes. It is often based on a critique of the capitalist mode of production and how different disciplines approach political economy through the lens of their subject's world view. Issues such as power and the inequality that stems from the capitalist system are analysed, to highlight how resource allocation can cause and perpetuate inequality and affect the public good. One approach used to justify public sector intervention is that of addressing market failures, where the local state seeks to address system failure in attending to the social welfare needs of the population. Here the frame of analysis is often conditioned by the disciplinary perspective or different approaches to political economy, such as the new institutional economics with its focus on institutions and alternative governance models. From an institutional perspective, one participant described the central–local government relationship as being in a constant state of flux (Dollery and Wallis 2001) and described the state's shortcomings in the following terms:

> *Since 2010 there's been no national strategy on ageing at a governmental level [. . .] it's in permanent crisis mode isn't it. And then public health [. .] is best defined really by somebody like Michael Marmot. So, Marmot produces a series of eye-catching reports [. . .] which are great reports that everybody loves, but doesn't mention anything about ageing in them. So, you've got a profession, a public health profession that isn't that interested in ageing or older people, because it's too late by then. So [. . .] what I would say is you've got a gap between if you like the health and care gaze, which looks at that top 5–10% of people, [and] a public health gaze which stops thinking about people generally speaking once they get to a certain age in terms of their*

strategy. So, you've got this gap in-between those two gazes, and that's where our work comes in[,] I think where I would argue, it's a kind of citizenship, sociological, I don't know, whatever you want to describe it, there's a number of ways, gerontological ways of describing the work that we do, or it's informed by those things. So, I think on the one hand there's this kind of conceptual issue and organisational issue, structural issue, and then on the other hand, you've[,] if you like[,] big politics [. . .] I remember being sat there maybe in about 2011, XXXX undergoing huge cuts, 40% cuts or something like that, it's a battlefield really out there. We're making huge cuts in lots of services that aren't statutory services that older people would rely on, particularly in low-income neighbourhoods and communities. It's a kind of a story not being told actually about the impact of all that I think on ageing populations, or not adequately told maybe . . . so we gathered together through a shared network of people who were kind of into this stuff, you know the enthusiasts, and a number of us got together and we ended up launching this UK network of age-friendly cities. So, we used the WHO model as a way of insulating us from big politics, you know, it wasn't a New Labour programme, it wasn't a coalition programme, it was [a] WHO Geneva programme. So, a bit of a flag of convenience, a reasonably good conceptual framework, and that's really the story. [P13]

This interpretation of the emergence and development of the age-friendly programme in the UK offers a pragmatic and political-economy perspective on how the development was a reaction to major political cuts to services for an ageing population, and how this was then rebranded and reinvented through the age-friendly lens. It also reiterates the need to fill a void left by a national public health policy that is rather myopic about ageing, even though from a life-course perspective – which the public health profession actually utilises – this leads to omitting from consideration up to half many peoples' life course. This perspective is also interconnected with arguments around the invisibility of ageing as a major theme by some participants alongside the obvious threat to public services posed by funding cuts.

Summary

This chapter has sought to relay and narrate many of the informative stories and perspectives offered by participants about why some localities chose the AFC journey and how this came about. No two localities have followed identical development paths, and in reality the diversity of development models means that their complexity is such that we cannot fully do justice to them in this summary format. The story behind each locality is unique and nuanced but some very clear similarities and differences emerge in those trajectories. A wide range of factors have shaped the development paths and specific formats of the AFC in each locality, including the way each programme was formulated and championed. However, this chapter has only begun to share the stories of the experiences of the AFCs in the UK, and so the next chapter continues by exploring a series of themes that help to understand their operation, achievements and progress in specific areas.

4 The reach, impact and implementation of age-friendly communities in the UK

Introduction

In the previous chapter, our analysis of the evolution and expansion of age-friendly schemes highlighted the effect of specific factors that contributed to the diversity of locality experiences. It examined how age-friendly policy had been formulated and championed (see McGarry and Morris 2011; Menec et al. 2013) including the types of innovations adopted in communities (see Lehning 2012; Ravi et al. 2021; van Hoof et al. 2019) and recognising the challenges of living in a digital world (Prendergast and Garattini 2015; Reuter et al. 2020) and the lived experience of being an older citizen in a city (van Hoof et al. 2022). Each participant highlighted the critical role of establishing and maintaining a dialogue with older residents and local communities. This chapter will expand upon some of the challenges that participants highlighted in terms of extending the reach of the programme and deepening the interactions with older people. It will also focus on the actions and investments made as well as the interactions developed with businesses, using the case of the visitor economy, which many older residents and visitors interact with as part of their leisure lives. One of the most widely discussed themes by participants was the issue of communication. Communication is critical to all aspects of the age-friendly model, which begins with a baseline assessment of information and community needs and involves consultation and active citizen engagement. The Covid pandemic added further complexity to this process, as many participants highlighted how this had reduced their ability to reach certain groups and compounded issues of social isolation.

Communicating with older residents: A perennial challenge?

As it is a community-based development model, local government is key to age-friendliness, which is significant in the light of the renaissance in the

DOI: 10.4324/9781003319801-4

role of the local state, identified by Nabatchi and Amsler (2014). The local state has an all-encompassing role and the community is the focus of its work, which spans the delivery of public services and goods, their improvement and targeting to groups in need of their provision. The local state also plays a fundamental role in

> building community, and generating support, agreement, and momentum for public actions to more philosophical concerns about remediating democratic and citizenship deficits, addressing complex governance problems and taking advantage of transformations in the expectations and capacities of ordinary people. Buttressing these and other raisons d'être is the evolution of information, communication, and other technologies that have made large-scale public engagement more feasible and potentially more productive than ever before. (Nabatchi and Amsler 2014: 645)

This quotation also illustrates the inextricable link between local government and community; here, the connection between government and real-world issues is more easily identified as it represents the 'most permeable region of government; it is more proximate and accessible to individuals' (Nabatchi and Amsler 2014: 645). The challenge lies in translating Nabatchi and Amsler's (2014) arguments into reality, so local people can engage with and co-produce the age-friendly programme.

The literature on engagement and local government suffers from a lack of clarity around the terminology used, with Nabatchi and Amsler (2014) pointing to multiple terms that are often used interchangeably. For the age-friendly programme, the most appropriate terminology is 'public engagement [which] refers to a variety of in-person and online methods for bringing people together to address issues of public importance' (Nabatchi and Amsler 2014: 655). The age-friendly model in its generic form is a form of public interaction which seeks to bring the lay public and other groups together through multiple modes of engagement that use different communication channels. The commonly used tools include public meetings; remoter modes of gathering community views, such as mail or web-based surveys; focus groups; online tools, like chatrooms; and networking with interested organisations.

One of the most useful landmark studies on public engagement from a planning perspective was Arnstein's (1969) critical interpretation, which conceptualised it as a *ladder of citizen participation* (Figure 4.1). This helps us understand how we might build a culture of citizen participation in age-friendly programme development, and highlights ways to overcome non-participation. As Arnstein (1969: 216) explained, 'there is a crucial difference between going through the empty ritual of participation and having real power to affect the outcome of the process'. Consequently, Arnstein identified three categories of participation: degrees of citizen power; degrees of tokenism; and non-participation. One of the roadblocks to full participation was the question of how and where to access the voices of those who are less willing or able to normally participate due to poor knowledge or low levels of education. Achieving a representation of the community also requires an understanding of the politics of local communities, as well as relationship building and establishing trust with the community. Studies such as Gilroy (2005) suggest that the older population places a higher value on information than other groups in helping form decisions, even though their access to information is often poor. Gilroy (2005) views information as an empowering tool, and in order to forge partnerships with local people to empower them, it is essential that stakeholders (e.g. AF programmes) can make information available to them through various conduits. In other words, information needs to be disseminated in a usable

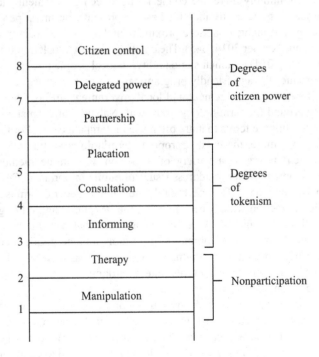

Figure 4.1 Eight rungs on a ladder of citizen participation

Source: Arnstein (1969: 217)

form to help older people make informed choices and to help them express their views about things that affect them. Therefore, how did participants communicate with their publics (i.e. residents, local organisations and businesses) as part of the age-friendly development process?

Participants' perspectives on communicating with older people

One theme that emerged in the narratives was that the principles of participatory policymaking, as outlined by Michels and De Graaf (2010, 2017), are a positive aspect of democratic decision-making in communities. Participants emphasised the importance of encouraging engagement and of the implementation of outreach (directly and via third-party organisations to encourage greater engagement) at an early stage of the policymaking process. The use of community organisations to help with reaching residents was paramount. As one participant emphasised, 'we needed the leadership to drive it forward and certainly at a community level, community leadership, otherwise again it's seen as the Council coming to do things to people' [P7]. What is also evident is the lengths participants went to in order to overcome the concerns voiced by Michels and De Graaf (2010: 489) about the 'exclusion of certain groups in that some quiet voices are never heard, which may eventually contribute to lowering public trust in government and a diminishing quality of democracy'. In the case of a national agency leading an age-friendly programme, these traits were seen as particularly important. In the words of one participant, 'there is also a need to ensure that representation is present from all communities and older people are involved . . . everybody has an opportunity . . . How can we ensure that this is as diverse and representative as it possibly can be so that nobody gets left behind, and everybody . . . has an opportunity to contribute and share their own experiences and participate in how that moves forward[?]' [P19]. Elements of this line of argument were also reiterated by the following participant, who argued that accessing harder to reach people was a

> *perennial challenge . . . a lot of what we want to do is to address . . . inequalities really, and it's for an organisation which is about the voice of older people, it's getting beyond the people who have the confidence to speak up, who can be very articulate about what's going on in their lives, or the issues as they see them, it's to get beyond that and to engage with people who still have plenty to say, but wouldn't easily come forward in that way. So it's developing processes of engagement I think that are more accessible and easier for people to engage with, so that actually you're getting a diverse voice. [P9]*

Another participant endorsed this approach but also highlighted the problem of operationalising a community-based approach from a local authority perspective because of funding cuts:

> *We've had cuts, cuts in terms of budgets but you know, many years ago we would have had community development officers whose job would have been to . . . get in that community and understand that community and that community's voice, so we have an age-friendly . . . group which is a community in XXXX and that was kind of what our plan was[,] to try and have more community-based groups driven by the communities.* [P9]

These apposite quotations are a useful starting point for an analysis of how participants utilised different communication channels to reach their publics. Figure 4.2 summarises the channels used. One method was face-to-face engagement (e.g. public meetings and more distant methods using the resources of other organisations with access to large memberships). Information communication technologies were also used (e.g. email, websites,

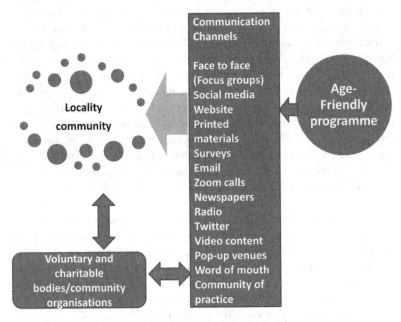

Figure 4.2 Communication channels used by age-friendly programmes

video calls and social media) and hard copies of the material were posted out or dropped off at key access points in the community (e.g. supermarkets, chemists, community centres). The following three quotations provide a useful overview of how these communication channels were used simultaneously:

> *We try to communicate via our offline publication that reaches doorsteps . . . as well as sharing via . . . radio, via community groups and services that support and work with residents and online via our newsletters and social media.* [P24]
>
> *I sit on the XXXX Network which is an umbrella group of older people's groups within our council area. A lot of information goes out through them. We do use social media and email contacts but because 58% of our residents aged 65+ have never accessed the internet . . . we also use a variety of other means. I have a database of approx. 70 older people's groups that I post information to on a regular basis, we do press releases in local papers, produce and print newsletters for distribution, and leave flyers in popular places that older people use (i.e. Post Office).* [P27].

Even so, as one participant candidly explained:

> *we haven't solved the problem about how we communicate effectively, we might communicate to a small number of our residents but not to everyone, I mean we work very closely with our equalities and diversity colleagues, they sit in our team, so they're very good at . . . trying to get messages out to perhaps our BAME communities, seldom heard communities, but again it's how you make sure that the communication is relevant to that community, so it can't be one size fits all.* [P7]

Herein lies the challenge of taking an idealised model of community-based age-friendliness and then putting it into practice, as the real world is complex, and there are no simple solutions to community engagement. Any engagement needs to be able to demonstrate cognitive and social empathy, and ideally, an empathetic concern which is likely to show the recipients that you want to help them. Therefore, trust and empathy in communication are reinforced by working with trusted partners when local authorities lead the age-friendly process, as the following quotation indicates:

> *We do use social media, but obviously, we know that's not for everybody. We do telephone and we do letters as well. We also work really,*

really closely with our voluntary sector and they're just really good at communicating. We have an older people's platform, so we often go to the older people's platform to get views and understand . . . but I think for the majority of people that we're trying to reach, we're not getting to them. But having said that, that's partially because of Covid. [P10]

The problem of Covid has added an additional layer of complexity, but one of the more established age-friendly communities did reinforce the trust built up through working with organisations outside of the council:

We've got a really strong third sector and we've got neighbourhood networks, so we've got 37 neighbourhood networks that basically cover the geographical area of the city, but they're very, very local organisations that understand their communities really, really well, and I think a lot of our work is done through the third sector so they're the trusted, they've got the trusted relationships, they've got the communication channels to get to the people that we would like to be communicating with, so often we will go through them, but equally it's two-way because we often go to them to kind of gather the insight from those particular communities so that we can use that to inform our work. We've got lots and lots of different kind of communication channels that we use, and actually, I think one of the great things, if you can say it that way, of Covid is that although it has widened the digital divide for some communities, a lot more older people have become savvier online and they are now accessing things that perhaps they wouldn't have done before, which again enables us to communicate with them in a different way. [P17]

Community groups and engagement

Community and voluntary groups were used by age-friendly leads as an innovative method of having a physical presence to encourage face-to-face engagement. One participant described how they might pop up

in a disused retail unit in the local shopping centre, or the library, or the market . . . we're quite often giving out information because we'll tell partners that we're there, and they'll say, 'Oh could you hand out these flyers about' . . . so it turns into a sort of hub of useful information activity, people come up to us . . . we try and have partners there as well, so the local volunteer bureau might be there, Age UK will come, Carers XXXX, XXXX District Council, Citizens Advice, and

> *Royal Voluntary Service, so it becomes . . . [a] useful interagency chat places, as well as interacting with the public* [P2]

These types of arrangements also worked well for the baseline study phase in some of the age-friendly localities and reflecting upon this, another participant observed that the challenge was in 'having multiple perspectives . . . it's quite easy to talk to older people who're sitting in a daycare centre and we did some of that, or people who were accessing community-based services, but also we wanted to talk to people . . . [with] . . . a range of incomes, we wanted to talk to people who had a range of life experiences, and talk to some of the younger and fitter cohort that might not see themselves in that older person category, and actually they were probably the hardest for us to reach' [P14].

But a key question is about the scope and scale of engagement achieved through the different communication methods. Several participants were able to quantify this, for example:

> *we do use digital, but we're very conscious that a large number of older people will not have access to the internet . . . we have an e-bulletin, which is a monthly newsletter, which goes out to just under 10,000 people. That carries a range of information around what's going on, advice, research, webinars, events, activities. We have the Age-Friendly . . . Twitter account, pre-Covid we'd agreed that we'd do two newspapers a year . . . it's kind of a tabloid-sized . . . newspaper . . . we distribute it through our networks, so our colleagues in libraries, well, they were shut, our housing providers, our neighbourhood workers, community groups, they all take copies and get them into people's hands. So we have done 18,000 copies in the winter '19 edition and they were distributed, as I say, through a range of organisations . . . we put 10,000 into the 20 main supermarkets . . . around the time of the first wave, [in conjunction with a regional age-friendly organisation] they did a keeping well at home booklet . . . we put some money into that and we distributed . . . about 15,000. We mailed out, through the council, a copy to everybody aged over 70 in the city. And that was part of our emergency response to the city around Covid, our mutual aid hub response . . . we contributed towards the . . . Keeping Well This Winter booklet . . . about 35,000 copies went out in XXXX. [P5]*

This participant reinforces the very important message, which came up frequently in the responses, that different communication channels need to be targeted in parallel to get to the hard-to-reach populations.

The digital divide

The role of digital technology may be a valuable way to reach older people, according to White and Verdusco (2018) as technology may help in bridging sensory changes in later life among the technology-literate. In contrast, Arnold and Boggs (2019) outline many of the special communication needs of older residents, and a key consideration is that many have an aversion to new technologies and to new ways of doing things. Hofmann et al. (2013) noted that as residents do not always make use of digital opportunities, the digital option has to be a complementary route to public engagement alongside more traditional methods of engaging with the local community. Nevertheless, de Mello (2021) suggested that engagement with the community increases throughout the later stages of the life cycle, as older people feel more attached to and part of their local community. Other studies have highlighted the rise of e-government and the online revolution, these have not supplanted the need for a diversity of communication channels for local government bodies to reach their publics (e.g. Firmstone and Coleman 2015; Sanders and Canel 2015). The challenge of Covid and ensuring older residents were not isolated led several participants to highlight the scale of digital engagement:

> *One of the big issues that we come across is around digital inclusion. So much of life is now on the internet and we know that, through Covid, only 35% of the people we were working with, so that was the people that didn't have social support or networks, only 35% of them were online at all.* [P16]

A leading charitable organisation involved in the age-friendly journey for a major city argued that

> *the three biggest issues that have come up have been social isolation and the impact on wellbeing, digital exclusion and access to food. So our work for the next year or so is going to be based on those issues . . . we're going to campaign on digital exclusion, but the quickest way, quite frankly, at the moment that we can mobilise people is via online campaigning.* [P23]

The participant highlighted the paradox of the digital divide as the reach achieved through digital lobbying led by the organisation led to the following result: 'we managed to mobilise our supporters and . . . we got them to send 45,000 emails to the Transport Secretary in the two weeks' [P23].

Funding and investment

the discussion, but financial resources remain a key to the implementation of

Plate 4.1 The digital divide: Technology is a barrier for some older people, a proportion of whom have never used the internet

Plate 4.2 The role of technology may be a valuable way to reach older people, according to White and Verdusco (2018), as technology may help in bridging sensory changes in later life among the technology-literate

Source: ©Centre for Ageing Better 2022

Funding issues emerged throughout the interviews at various points in the discussion, but financial resources remain key to the implementation of the WHO model, particularly in the baseline and data-gathering stage (i.e. staff time and the process of community engagement). A leading participant in an age-friendly-city initiative shared their experience of how they negotiated this process, as well as the broader perspective of its Chief Officer:

> *he was a real advocate in the Council and beyond for age-friendly and has been talking about it for a very long time, so I think people see that . . . we have the kind of milestones that we've worked through to get to where we're at, and equally I think we can demonstrate the impact that it's had . . . I think funding always does help but equally there have been times where it's been a struggle to secure that funding and . . . [it] . . . is about the influence and how actually it needs to be cross-council, it needs to be across all partners within the city because it's not just public health's responsibility or just not one person's responsibility, it needs to be that collective effort, so I think we probably achieve a lot just through having that influencing role and really getting people to think with an older person's lens. [P17]*

This is reinforced in Table 4.1, which outlines the networked nature of the age-friendly relationships that participants mentioned explicitly (although in reality, the web of relationships is likely to be far denser and more complex than the table suggests). It also illustrates the issue of serendipity highlighted in Chapter 3. Table 4.1 represents many of the attributes discussed

Table 4.1 Networks of relationships and organisations the age-friendly programme works with

Third sector	Local authority	Other public sector	Transnational organisation	Private sector
Voluntary organisations	Social care	AgeWell boards (or equivalents)	World Health Organization	Crowdfunding
Community organisations	Planning	Social housing groups		Transport companies
Volunteer bureau	Fire brigade	National Health Service		Taxi companies
HealthWatch	Housing provision	Funded projects on ageing		Chamber of Commerce
Citizens Advice	Neighbourhood teams	Universities		Pharmacies
Age UK	District councils	Business improvement districts		Urban regeneration schemes

Third sector	Local authority	Other public sector	Transnational organisation	Private sector
Royal Voluntary Service	Greater London Authority	Devolved government departments (Wales and Northern Ireland)		
Alzheimer's Society	Cultural organisations (museums and theatres)			
Centre for Ageing Better				

in Chapter 2 in terms of the skills needed to implement the age-friendly programme. Nevertheless, a wide range of participants did point to the tight financial environment they were working in (including annual recurrent funding streams, even though the age-friendly commitment signs the locality up to a five-year commitment).

Participants were able to reflect upon the ongoing investment in their age-friendly programmes, and several approaches emerged (see Figure 4.3). The majority of participants had no immediate budget or relied upon project funding or exerting influence on other programmes of work to achieve their age-friendly objectives. The lack of budgetary resources to effect direct change indicates that the age-friendly paradigm does not simply rely on such sources, but is a mindset and approach to the public realm, as the following three quotations demonstrate:

> *This work is so under-funded, a lot of the time it is run on goodwill alone! There used to be a small budget attached that came from the main public health budget but that has since gone.* [P24]
>
> *There is no direct financial commitment attached to this strategy. This strategy is primarily about embedding age-friendly approaches and principles into existing programmes of work and creating culture change and transformation. Existing budgets will accommodate through embedding these principles through existing programmes of work, revised commissioning arrangements, partnership working . . . There are a number of key services that hold responsibility for actions committed.* [P25]
>
> *So there's some work going on around high streets at the moment. So we are again sitting around the table and helping to push the age-friendly agenda . . . we see an opportunity and*

then we put our hands up and say, 'we can help you to ensure the voice of older people involved in that'. So we don't go with a stick and say 'look, this pavement isn't safe. It needs to be X, Y and Z.' We did some really good work, particularly in the early days . . . to connect [local government] to older people to have those conversations. So we got some dropped curbs done, we got some bus shelters sorted out. We got some bits and pieces done. We've been using things like walking audits and that. So, obviously, using the public spaces particularly during Covid[,] using those parks to be able to show actually there's a lot of investment [that has] already happened in XXXX and how safe these spaces are. [P3]

What these quotations illustrate, as Hajnal and Trounstine (2010) suggest, is a complex set of parameters that impact local government spending, where economic imperatives dominate but a combination of political imperatives, institutional constraints, and actual needs also emerge. In short, 'local government spending decisions are more multifaceted than at least some previous accounts have suggested. Local government budgets are a function of a complex interplay of politics, economics, institutions, and basic needs' (Hajnal and Trounstine 2010: 1154) and so getting the age-friendly focus onto the agendas of different areas of spending is critical.

Where major changes occurred as a result of investments, participants were able to demonstrate changing practices, as summarised in Table 4.2. Table 4.2 lists a wide range of themes (the major changes) – and sub-themes

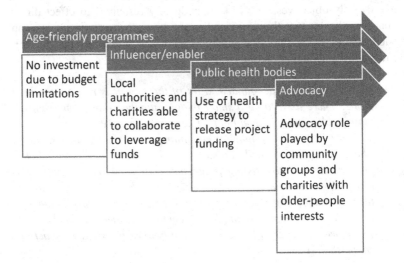

Figure 4.3 Methods of investment to develop age-friendly programmes

Table 4.2 Selected examples of changes introduced by the age-friendly programme

Major change	New practice	Evaluation
Working with Volunteer Community Support	Establishment of chatty cafes (to help reduce loneliness and isolation)	Discussions with café owners
	Take a Seat campaign for people when shopping	Discussion with retail sector to see if they are used
Enhanced communication with older people	Social radio run by the community sector with council support	Looking at the numbers engaged and how staff practices have changed, with a focus on equality issues
	Creation of child-friendly borough and how to create intergenerational spaces	Looking at the numbers engaged and how staff practices have changed, with a focus on equality issues
	Digital buddies and skills	Looking at the numbers engaged and how staff practices have changed, with a focus on equality issues
Digital exclusion	Digi Friends	
Service provision and infrastructure adaptations	Commissioned fire service to build falls prevention into their safe-and-well visits	Using age-friendly indicators which measure success in terms of WHO domains, public health outcomes framework, health and social care outcomes
	The council commissions AccessAble to undertake audits of public spaces and their accessibility; over 100 have been audits completed	
	Books at Home project for older residents who are unable to make independent visits to libraries. This has included creating volunteer opportunities to deliver the service	
	The needs of older people and those with disabilities are considered when planning all events, i.e. seating, signage, travel	

(Continued)

Table 4.2 (Continued)

Major change	New practice	Evaluation
	All new signal-controlled pedestrian crossings or those being upgraded have the latest 'Puffin Crossing' technology, installed to help ensure that pedestrians, particularly the mobility impaired, are given sufficient time to cross the highway safely. Older crossings that have not yet been upgraded have been given additional 'green' time to better facilitate slower pedestrians as they cross	
	All new housing developments in the city are assessed in terms of age-friendliness: priority is given to those that are planned for sustainable locations where there is access to GP surgeries, dentists and local shops and services	
Representation on major city regeneration project Older-person representation on two regeneration schemes	Influence priorities at an early stage to design in age-friendly priorities Ability to shape priorities	Potentially, Key Performance Indicators
Changes to business practice	Age-friendly retail scheme/ age-friendly business	
	Age-friendly business scheme	Older Person's Forum looking at feasibility and scope
	Age-friendly training for organisations	Following up with organisations to see what changes have been implemented
Undertaking the baseline assessment	Use of volunteers to undertake audits of facilities	

Major change	New practice	Evaluation
New concepts of city living	The 15-minute city with neighbourhoods and their residents having access to the bulk of their needs either by walking, cycling or using public transport within a 15-minute time frame	
New service provision and measures to raise a positive public image of ageing	Safer Homes initiative Handyman service Age-friendly business charter Awards for volunteers Positive Ageing Month Covid grants to help with grocery deliveries	Carrying out city resident satisfaction surveys and demand measures (e.g. the demand for handyman service outstripped supply)
Enhancing public transport access and provision	Age-friendly bus stops Developing a door-to-door service for the more isolated residents Influencing bus driver training	
Rural accessibility	Using the community infrastructure in rural areas Using Community Support Officers to engage with residents in remoter areas Working with a regional organisation that coordinates older groups	

(the new practices which had been introduced). A diversity of themes emerged that illustrate the enabling and influencing role of the age-friendly programme, with some of these themes discussed by several participants. The changes and practices illustrate how interventions were designed to make a difference in the ageing population's interactions with the built and natural environment. These were typically at specific touchpoints, ranging from the home environment to parks and open spaces, town centres, rural areas and access to public transport. In some instances, the evaluation had accompanied implementation, while in others it was still to occur. Some of the new practices were low cost and had involved partnership working in their implementation.

The politics of public-sector spending on age-friendly programmes typically reflects a hierarchical decision-making model where age-friendly officers or managers of programmes recommend their funding require-ments to their senior managers, often as part of annual budget plans. These are then passed upwards to budget holders, who then reject or propose them to the elected decision-makers overseeing the council's spending portfolio. A similar process, albeit a less complex one, also applies to charities. But as Chapter 3 illustrated, other factors impact on funding decisions such as party politics, the careers of individual politicians, and those politicians' interest in ageing and ability to influence public resource allocation (Dan-ziger 1978). The quotations above on funding and investment reinforce the arguments by Everingham et al. (2012) on how important partnerships were in creating a common agenda to influence investment outcomes. Warner and Zhang (2021) supported these claims, illustrating that cross-ageing collaborations were important to promote the age-friendly pro-gramme in areas the programme lead did not control. One other way to leverage investment, as noted by de Widt (2021), was by demonstrating cost savings or a beneficial social benefit using Social Return on Invest-ment methodologies (SROI). SROI quantifies the broader social, economic and environmental value of a defined investment, as in the example given by one participant:

> *We're participating with the University of Cambridge in some research around the return on investment for age-friendly, . . . the end goal is that . . . investment in this area has a positive result, positive SROI, and therefore we can justify spending more money.* [P8]

Therefore, making sound financial cases for investment in a constrained finan-cial environment was shown to be essential to promoting age-friendly work.

Environmental improvements

One area of investment which Handler (2014) highlighted was in the environmental improvements made to adapt the existing environments to accommodate the needs of ageing users, as well as to improve design fea-tures for all. New York City (NYC) is an interesting case in point illustrat-ing how one large city approached this. NYC focused on accessibility and safety: 'some of the improvements made by Age-Friendly NYC include a reduction in senior pedestrian fatalities by 21%, increased walkability through the addition of public seating, new programming for older people at parks, educational and cultural institutions, and a better consumer experience offered by many local businesses' (Goldman et al. 2016: 171). The justification for intervention on seating provision in the built environment was highlighted by many of the participants: 'long-term conditions from 55 plus come in, because if you've got heart disease, COPD, diabetes, obesity . . . and suddenly your ability to walk far without resting is compromised, so that's where Aging Well comes in. And as you get older, obviously your mobility can decline anyway . . . So you need age-friendly benches' [P5]. Achieving these changes can require community-wide strategies to be put in place, as the following quotation suggests:

> *The City Plan includes a number of commitments which support inclusive design . . . From 1 April 2021 at least 10% of new dwellings are accessible and adaptable . . . ensuring there is a choice of suitable accommodation for older people.* [P26]

Where one age-friendly lead had prioritised benches, the development process used volunteers to audit their provision:

> *we had a map on the council page which had the benches . . . we got a community group involved . . . who committed to run or, well, basically run every street of XXXX. So I provided them with maps of what we currently knew, where the current benches were. They marked whether they were still there, but they also marked whether they were age-friendly. So, for example, did they have a back, did they have arms so that you could lift yourself up, . . . what condition they were in. And so we've added some new keys to the council mapping system, so we've colour coded it for the age-friendly ones . . . that . . . enables me to . . . produce ward-based reports that . . . identify where the benches are within their wards, which ones need repairing. And it also creates the functionality of being able to mark on the map where suggested new benches [should be placed].* [P21]

This was then fed to the ward-related budget holders for action. In the case of public toilet provision, as Participant 7 suggested, 'public toilets is an issue that seems to be inherent you know, in my work I think we've always had the challenge around public toilets . . . accessibility of toilets'. Thinking laterally to find solutions that are cost neutral led one participant to argue that

> *people are also saying that they need toilets and there's not many public toilets in XXXX. But we don't necessarily think building new*

public toilets is necessarily the answer, because there's hundreds of toilets available in XXXX . . . if you count all the pubs, large retail outlets and restaurants . . . is there not a different way that we can do this, working in partnership with businesses? . . . Kendal in the Lake District have a courtesy toilet scheme, where they've got various businesses that help to raise their PR by saying, 'We're people friendly. If you need to use our toilet, that's absolutely fine, you don't need to be a customer.' [P21]

This novel approach was reinforced by Participant 10, who also saw it as part of the wider remit of how 'awareness-raising works when you're working with planning colleagues, when you're working with developers. The more awareness you raise, the more people will take it on board to make changes' [P10]. The approach was particularly important in terms of future development projects like the provision of new housing and in one locality, an initiative looking at the existing housing stock to ensure safer homes with free house visits (Table 4.2), and the introduction of a handyman service to help make changes or improvements and repairs. One other participant also discussed at length the national and local debates on 'rightsizing' and helping older people to ensure their housing met their needs (i.e. the housing had the necessary adaptations and was accessible). This was important given the issues of falls and accidents within the home among the ageing population (see Page and Connell 2022). In some cases, partners in the age-friendly initiative joined together to bid for funding (including the Centre for Ageing Better), such as by linking to agendas on frailty, and those on transport, to overcome issues of social isolation. One of the areas in which the age-friendly family, as it was described by several participants, could be extended was through advocacy as a way to offset funding issues.

Advocacy

Advocacy is an underpinning concept in the age-friendly movement. Advocacy has a key role in drawing attention to those with specific needs that are not being met. According to Gray, Kaslow and Allbaugh (2020: 2), 'Advocacy has long been characterized as the process of giving voice to those without voice or whose voices are not heard, which are often individuals served by and/or serving in public service settings.' Therefore, it has particular salience here for a community-focused initiative seeking to engage a wider range of publics and to build a growing movement of people able to recognise its virtues and relevance. This was represented in many of the narratives in terms of adopting an age-friendly lens as the following comments demonstrate:

> *so that age-friendly lens I talk about, I walk round the world and I see it in a different way because I've just learnt to, you know . . . it's interesting how, once you rope people in and work with them, and they join the family, the age-friendly family, as we call it . . . they start to see the world a bit like that as well. You know, the same way you see that around other equalities issues, you know, around disability and accessibility.* [P5]

Gray et al. (2020) argue that advocacy of this type, can help in achieving equity and justice for populations in public service settings. Participants were asked about the types of advocacy that might help with their age-friendly work, and the ways in which it could be used. One welcome finding was the widely endorsed success of the Centre for Ageing Better's Age-Friendly Community of Practice which helped share knowledge and experiences. As one participant suggested, it helped avoid reinventing the wheel. Other forms of advocacy included those identifying local research needs, such as the need to seek a better understanding of isolation and loneliness among vulnerable groups, evaluate how interventions in the age-friendly programme had worked, and to pursue research that progressed the equalities agenda so that minority groups were not excluded. One important area that the age-friendly WHO model only deemed to be a secondary priority was the area of business. To examine this issue further, this study frames the discussion of business interactions with the age-friendly programmes in terms of one of the UK's expanding areas of service sector activity – the visitor economy, especially as many residents (and visitors) are likely to have a degree of engagement with it in their leisure time.

Older residents and leisure time

The literature on ageing has a well-established pedigree of examining older people's leisure, particularly the relationship between retirement and the expansion of leisure time (Patterson 2018; Page and Connell 2022). In the UK, those aged over 65 have on average over 7 hours of leisure time a day, which for those with the financial resources, mobility and absence of barriers to participation provides a myriad of daily opportunities for at-home and out-of-home leisure activities in the community and further afield. Physical activity has long been seen as a factor that helps older people to age well. The Covid pandemic had a severe impact on patterns of leisure involving out-of-home physical activity, confining older people to their home environments and accentuating patterns of social isolation and loneliness, as the narratives have shown. As Public Health England (2021: 9) observed, the pandemic contributed to 'deconditioning – the loss of psychological, physical and functional capacity due to inactivity' and to a rise in falls as strength and balance were impacted, disproportionately affecting those from more deprived areas, who tended to be less active. Significant spatial inequalities in leisure exist among older people in terms of access to the leisure opportunities that are deemed important in ageing well, maintaining a good quality of life and accessing out-of-home leisure to overcome social isolation and loneliness. As Page and Connell (2022) illustrate, economic inequalities, even among the baby-boomer generation of older people, create *haves* and *have-nots*; this is reflected in the types of leisure opportunities which older people can access within their communities (e.g. clubs, societies and group activities) and those that involve interaction with the visitor economy.

The visitor economy: An area for development?

The visitor economy has substantial long-term growth prospects for the UK (Local Government Association 2013b), which has transitioned to a service economy, and many localities have highlighted the potential role of the visitor economy in achieving economic recovery in the UK post-pandemic. Barclays' (2015) report on hidden consumer spending among the ageing population found that UK hospitality businesses derived 20% of their turnover from those aged over 65, yet only 5% of businesses saw this as an important market. Therefore, the ageing population represents a hidden opportunity for the visitor economy and is a potential source of help with localised post-pandemic recovery strategies. The term 'visitor economy' is widely used as a surrogate for tourism and visitor activity within the public sector (see Page and Connell 2022). This has a political dimension to it as a measure of the visitor economy in localities is deemed to be higher when combining day-visitor and tourism spending and associated sectors, which helps leverage further public-sector support. Connell et al. (2017: 111), building upon a report by Barclays (2015), developed the following definition of the visitor economy:

> *It embraces the hospitality and tourism sector (food and drink provision via cafes, restaurants and accommodation), travel agencies, transport providers, cultural activities like galleries, events and retailing. There is often a blurring of the terms visitor economy, tourism and leisure as residents may also use the facilities and services in their leisure time. The term broadly refers to the supporting infrastructure that caters for the needs of visitors and residents, especially in their leisure time and so is very wide-ranging in what is included in such a categorisation.*

This definition shows the sheer scale and scope of the sector, especially when the visitor elements are disaggregated in order to illustrate how dependent some localities are on this form of income for local employment, given its highly seasonal nature (excluding many larger cities that have a significant business travel market that is less seasonal). It is also a key part of the leisure infrastructure of a locality, which is often described as the cultural industries. To illustrate the economic value of the sector in the localities included in this study, Table 4.3 compiles the latest data (pre-pandemic, as a surrogate of the visitor economy in a more normal operating environment) which illustrates the scale of activity, ranging from large cities down to smaller rural communities and represents a significant sector of most age-friendly communities in terms of opportunities as a setting for leisure activities and employment.

Table 4.3 The visitor economy in selected age-friendly communities, January 2021*

Place	County/Province	Estimates of visitor numbers per annum (day visitors, domestic and international tourists) in millions
Liverpool City Region	Merseyside	67.8
London Borough of Hackney	Greater London	(1)
Antrim and Newtownabbey	Ulster	0.1
Fermanagh and Omagh District	Ulster	0.4
Sheffield	South Yorkshire	17.2
Bristol	City of Bristol, Avon	25
Newry, Mourne and Down	Ulster	0.25
Metropolitan Borough of Sefton	Merseyside	10
London	Greater London Authority	41
Lisburn and Castlereagh	Ulster	0.2
Ards and North Down Borough	Ulster	0.3
Cheshire West and Chester Borough	Cheshire	36.4
Greater Manchester Combined Authority	Greater Manchester	57.8

(Continued)

Table 4.3 (Continued)

Place	County/Province	Estimates of visitor numbers per annum (day visitors, domestic and international tourists) in millions
Coventry	West Midlands	10
Derry City and Sherbourne	Ulster	1.02
Isle of Wight	Isle of Wight	2.7
Salford	Greater Manchester	1+
Sunderland	Tyne and Wear	9
Liverpool	Merseyside	40.7
London Borough of Southwark	Greater London	(1)
Newcastle upon Tyne	Tyne and Wear	18.65
Glasgow	Lanarkshire	32
Nottingham	Nottinghamshire	21.97
Manchester	Greater Manchester	57.8
Belfast	Ulster	4.7
Stoke-on-Trent	Staffordshire	1.3
Leeds	West Yorkshire	29
Brighton and Hove	East Sussex	11
Wales	Wales	96
Armagh	Ulster	0.18
York	Yorkshire	8.4
Oxfordshire	Oxfordshire	3.8+ (excludes Oxford, with 7 million a year)
Birmingham	Greater Birmingham Metropolitan area	41
Trafford	Greater Manchester	1+
London Borough of Sutton	London	(1)
Melksham	Wiltshire	No data
Hebden	North Yorkshire	No data
Barnsley	West Yorkshire	3
Bolton	Greater Manchester	No data
Middlesbrough	North Yorkshire	9.1
Torbay	Devon	5.2

+ This is an estimate from visitor attraction data as Greater Manchester data is not disaggregated down to locality

(1) Part of the Greater London data and not disaggregated to the London Boroughs.
Source: Centre for Ageing Better contacts list; various sources

* When the list was compiled, there were 41 age-friendly coordinator/contacts on the Centre for Ageing Better website. By April 2021 this had been further updated to include East Lindsey, Yale, Hastings, Wigan and North Yorkshire in order to recognise all 46 localities that were on the AF journey.

Engagement with the visitor economy

Participants discussed a wide range of facets of engagement with the visitor economy (see Table 4.4). However, many did not see differentiating between visitors and residents as important in the age-friendly planning process. As the participants stated:

> *No, we'd not thought about visitors, actually, but . . . if you adapt something for an older resident, it benefits not just the residents, but also visitors and also those who are under 65 who have, you know, particular physical or mental need[s]. [P1]*
>
> *I think people's needs are the same[:] whether you're a resident or whether you're a visitor[,] you still need exactly the same thing. [P3]*

Table 4.4 Age-friendly engagement with the visitor economy by localities

Activity/touchpoints with the local visitor economy	*Number of touchpoints*
No interactions	3
Business-friendly scheme/business charter/use of an auditing approach	8
Involvement with a destination management organisation or council-funded tourism body or visitor organisation	6
Regeneration scheme such as Business Improvement District (BID)	6
Engagement with a visitor attraction or museum	3
Engagement with culture network, art gallery or theatre	2
Engagement with transport providers (e.g. coach or bus company), public transport operator or promotional campaign with operator (e.g. ferry operator)	9
Engagement with hotels/cafes	4
Connection with Dementia-Friendly Scheme (either directly as an area of responsibility or indirectly as a partner)	6
Working relationship with the Chamber of Commerce	5
Engagement with specific infrastructure investments (typically cross-Council)in relation to	
• Community toilets	3
• Benches/seating/walkability/cycling	4
• Retailers/markets	3
Older People's Forums who were working on the visitor economy	3
Planning to pursue this area in the future (post-covid)	7

Number of localities: 28; number of mentions do not sum as some localities mentioned more than one form of engagement

This reinforces the case for thinking about the specific needs of visitors that may be aided by developments in age-friendly infrastructure. Despite these comments, the needs of visitors and residents are different, as reaffirmed by Walmsley and Jenkins (1992), who identified the time it takes visitors staying in a city to develop a mental map to navigate and wayfinding in a city. This is, typically, several days with supporting information and maps, depending on their unfamiliarity with the locality. When considering ageing visitors, other factors such as a potential decline in cognitive abilities, challenges in wayfinding and more mobility-related issues mean that visitor environments have to be designed with these issues in mind: signage and routeways become critical. In contrast, residents have more time and familiarity to work out the most suitable routeways. What was interesting from several participants' responses was the statement that they had no visitor economy or viewed it as an issue to progress in future, for example:

> *We're not a tourist destination.* [P16]
> *So, no, we haven't done that. It's something we'd like to do, certainly. You know, we've done it in the world of culture . . . but not across the wider business sector, certainly.* (P13)

But as Table 4.2 shows, most of the localities seeking to become age-friendly are visitor destinations of varying sizes and so this may well be a misunderstanding on the part of participants about the significance of this sector to their locality. One explanation of these responses was that participants were relying upon another agency (e.g. a council's economic development department or a charity) to progress more business-facing issues, as the following quotation suggests: '. . . our partner, XXXXXX are leading some work around age-friendly businesses' [P17].

In one case, the visitor economy was not on the agenda because:

> *the challenge or the problem is that that group of people [leading age-friendly] tend to think about the opportunities in terms of health, services, housing maybe a little bit, and I keep banging on to them about tourism.* [P13]

In some cases, localities had developed age-friendly business schemes that might encompass visitor businesses, by developing their own or modifying other age-friendly toolkits/checklists that could be used as a self-managed process for the business. Yet, with some exceptions (e.g. Stroud and Walker 2012), creating age-friendly business practices has not permeated the business literature to any great degree, so knowledge continues to rely upon the grey literature, as Chapter 2 indicated. Where age-friendly business schemes had been established, they had not been evaluated to assess their effectiveness or whether their objectives had been achieved, and were often framed as initiatives to promote innovation or to address a specific local issue. Several participants suggested developing age-friendly business schemes could be a useful way to help with post-Covid business recovery; as Participant 12 commented, 'there's a whole new world there where age-friendly is going to be involved with the recovery group which covers the local business forum' [P12].

One urban age-friendly leader pointed to the 60,000 visitors a day who had visited the locality's Saturday markets even during the pandemic, which supports this argument for thinking about the visitor economy as a focus for age-friendly actions. But even where age-friendly business schemes are promoted, the key is in explaining the shared value for the business; this concept was popularised by Porter and Kramer (2011) as a way of bringing business and society together, as Connell and Page (2019b) illustrated in the case of dementia-friendly communities. Porter and Kramer (2011: 5) identified three ways in which shared value could occur: by reconceiving markets and products; the redefinition of productivity in the value chain; and enabling cluster development. Each of these three approaches can be developed with the visitor economy, as one participant recognised the underlying premise of shared value: 'you've got to have the business case upfront to them to show if you do this this is what it's going to do to your turnover, then they're onboard' [P13].

One way of encouraging shared value, as has been evident in many of the examples in Table 4.4, is in how changes to business practices have occurred. Taking the example of becoming dementia-friendly, Connell and Page (2019a) demonstrated how Destination Management Organisations (DMOs) might lead this strand of work. In several localities, age-friendly initiatives were connected with such organisations, for example:

> *Visit XXXX is a Community Interest Company . . . it's absolutely . . . age-friendly XXXX and . . . one of the directors of that is one of our leadership group members* [P2]

and

> *Visit XXXX . . . are very clear that our ageing demographic is high here . . . they are very aware of the needs of older people . . . so I think we probably are a bit ahead in other areas. . . .* [P22]

One additional route to engaging with a DMO was through a local Business Improvement District (BID), a scheme where a rate is levied on local businesses to develop projects of benefit to the business community with support from central government, a successor to the Town Centre Management Schemes of the 1990s (Page and Hardyman 1996). Some DMOs have switched to this model of destination development to access more funding, and tourism BIDs have been established within the wider population of the 200 BIDs operating in the UK. Participant 2 noted the shift from DMO to BID: 'with XXXX BID, they have a shopping app which they are suggesting we might fiddle about with and it would become a toilet map app . . . and we would also do a toilet map as some other age-friendly communities have as well, a physical map . . . and have them in tourist information or wherever else' [P2].

This quotation also highlights a very controversial issue for an ageing demographic – the need to access public toilets. The frequency of urinating, as Bichard and Knight (2011) outlined, often increases as a result of ageing. Some innovative schemes, such as community-run toilets, have been promoted by age-friendly schemes, as discussed earlier. This was evident in one age-friendly location with a well-developed tourism and day-visitor market, which had 'spent a lot of time with the Council talking about the accessibility of the coast for people, and having amenities at the coast, like the toilets' [P4].

The controversy around toilets arises from the cuts to public funding that led to a number of public toilets closing as highlighted in Chapter 3, with some councils resorting to charging to offset their running costs (Frizzell 2019). Constructive dialogue with both BIDs and local Chambers of Commerce was also cited in many localities as a way of helping to connect with local businesses, as in this example: 'we have a representative from the Chamber of Commerce on our age-friendly group, we have certainly tried to engage with anyone . . . [including] . . . business improvement district people . . . [to] . . . encourage them to embrace age-friendly in the work that they do' [P9].

Many of the respondents were able to point to cultural infrastructure developed by the local council for residents of cities, such as museums, art galleries and events, which also have salience for attracting visitors. For residents, cultural infrastructure was made more financially and physically accessible by offering discounted or free admission in some areas. For example, in one larger city, the respondent outlined how their strategy had operated: 'one of the bigger developments . . . that have come on the back of age-friendly, is actually the investment we put into cultural services, and age-friendly cultural services . . .' [P8].

This has synergies with attracting a visitor market as well and in developing the night-time economy. In one locality, city-centre hotels had low vacancy rates, and so the business case for making them age-friendly was seen as limited. Conversely, in the same city, the participant pointed to the paradox that they 'market to people who are in their 50s and 60s and maybe 70s by showing people photographs of people in their 40s enjoying themselves' [P13]. Another destination recognised the need to develop hotels as age-friendly infrastructure; as there had been a booming short-break market before lockdown,

> . . . we have enough hotels to hopefully facilitate all those people. New hotels popping up everywhere at the moment . . . it probably isn't a big area that we've really thought about, but it . . . definitely has potential with the silver dollar. . . . I definitely see it as a market, and I suppose a lot of them do the mid-week deals and things for over '50s and various things like that. I think definitely it's something that we could approach. [P15]

Here, the notion of the silver dollar was identified, an argument that has been advanced to highlight the economic benefits of an age-friendly industry. While few age-friendly officers had had specific conversations or interactions with the accommodation sector, some hospitality providers were being targeted, as one participant acknowledged: 'we were developing that next level as to what about those cafes and spaces that people go to socially to eat, and how age-friendly are they' [R3].

In one locality the concept of chatty cafes had been trialled; in each café, a 'Chatty Table' was provided, so customers could sit there if they were happy to chat and natter with other people. This initiative was created to help overcome the issues of isolation and loneliness that affect up to 25% of older people (Cacioppo and Patrick 2008).

Transport is a vital ingredient, which connects visitor demand with supply and facilitates the mobility of older visitors. In terms of local bus provision, several localities with a defined visitor economy had trained local bus-company staff to issue guidelines to their drivers as well as consulting with user groups and industry bodies to promote age-friendly thinking (e.g. encouraging bus drivers to provide time for older people to get seated before pulling away, and to help them with their luggage); 'from a transportation perspective [the aim was] to support tourism and helping people get around' [P22]. In one instance, the age-friendly locality created tourism-specific services to fill gaps in provision for tourists because 'there was no public transport to the seafront, it's not far, but it's too far if you find walking difficult, you know . . . [the local bus company put] . . . on a bus during the summer season to take people from the shopping area to the seafront' [P4]. Other measures included creating a 'set of standards for taxi drivers teaching them good practice when working with older people' [P24].

One development that several localities discussed was how their work on becoming dementia-friendly had seen a focus on making a crossover to become age-friendly (see Turner and Cannon 2018 for a discussion of aligning these two strands of 'friendly' activity within localities), as Participant 17 indicates:

> *if you've put in place the mechanisms to become a dementia-friendly community, many of the things that you will have done will reflect age-friendly practice as well . . . I think what we need to be cautious of is introduction of any notion of them as competing agendas . . . they are very complementary agendas and you know, just because you're dementia-friendly doesn't mean you cannot be age-friendly or vice versa.* [P17]

Yet, with the onset of Covid-19, most respondents had put engagement with visitor economy businesses on hold, or just planned to develop this area in future. For example, the following quotation shows the synergies that connect age-friendly initiatives with other accessible agendas:

> *in our strategy we have outlined commitment to engage with our business network and wider businesses in the borough through sharing a co-produced (yet to be developed) guide on what would make an age-friendly business and also to encourage a 'time to rest and pop to the loo' campaign where older residents can use the toilet/take a break without pressure of making a purchase. We are also keen that this guide is age-friendly, dementia-friendly, autism and LD [learning disabilities]-friendly.* [P25]

When asked about how organisations would progress the visitor economy agenda further, a range of approaches were outlined, including using local independent groups of over-50s, for example: 'we've got an age-friendly business guide, we've got resource[s] in XXXXXX Older People's Forum to . . . those businesses and support them to become more age-friendly, and we've linked age-friendly and dementia-friendly together, so it's more around friendly communities, so by becoming more age-friendly I suppose you're friendly for all ages' [P17].

Other age-friendly schemes focused on this as a future area that needed further work. One respondent recognised the logic of extending previous work on the visitor economy, mentioning that 'we were looking at chatty café schemes and how we could utilise those to support the visitor economy. And the hospitality industry . . . we've done some work around the night-time economy and, you know, don't just rule out older people because you think they want to be safely tucked up in bed at seven o'clock' [P7].

One locality acknowledged that a national steer was needed, and mentioned the importance of trade bodies, destination management and national tourism organisations in connecting the strands to help give a greater impetus and structure to managers of age-friendly schemes. Specifically, one participant outlined the need to look at 'how we engage with those bodies and organisations and also how we might engage with older people who are visiting as a group so that we could almost crosscheck my assumption that we are a city for all ages and therefore we would be meeting the needs of people visiting as well as living [there]' (P17). This observation has also been made by Connell and Page (2019b) in a discussion about dementia-friendly initiatives. Two undeveloped areas not explored by participants were the night-time economy and the day-visitor market. Some respondents did connect the visitor economy with post-Covid recovery and the potential of the silver dollar/pound, but few localities saw the marketing potential of ageing visitors to help create a tourism-led recovery. From the narratives, it was apparent that participants had not fully embraced the age-friendly business concept of the visitor economy so there is considerable scope for development, particularly as the approach advocated by some respondents was that what is good for the ageing population often equates to good for access for all, especially where Universal Design principles are embedded in the work. Many of the respondents were able to point to well-established programmes of work on ageing and exemplars of best practices (typically these age-friendly schemes were based on cities with larger populations, due to their greater resources).

Summary

From the narratives, key strands that emerged in the age-friendly narrative included a focus on creating documents (e.g. strategies/action plans) as well as on governance and resourcing, all characteristics of the public-sector approach. From our documentary analysis, the grey literature and examples cited in the interviews, it appears that those involved with the age-friendly agenda implicitly connect it with the visitor economy, but do not acknowledge the importance of localities. This reflects the social policy paradigm that shaped the participants' thinking informed by the WHO model of community development, a theme we discussed in Chapter 1. The social-policy focus is also reinforced through the public-sector ethos that permeates age-friendly initiatives, which have been implemented in a way that has shown limited engagement with private-sector businesses. That is not a criticism, as the narratives demonstrated a willingness among participants to look across disciplinary boundaries (e.g. social care and health) and to recognise the nascent potential of the visitor economy. However, many of the necessary elements are not in place or connected, so the community development model cannot embrace the economic development potential of becoming age-friendly or the opportunities of creating shared value to the fullest extent. There are some complementary infrastructure improvements whereby residents' and visitors' needs are synonymous (e.g. provision of benches, accessible streetscapes, buildings and toilet provision). But when looking at the visitor journey in these localities and the touchpoints of those visitors' experiences, a major chasm exists between a resident's leisure needs (e.g. access to a local park or a town-centre cultural facility) and the more in-depth wayfinding needs of a visitor population. Therefore, with these issues in mind, we turn to the final chapter, in which we outline the implications and conclusions that can be drawn from this study.

5 Where to next?

Critical reflections and prospects for age-friendly communities

Introduction

The primary research reported in Chapters 3 and 4 represented a selective assessment of the extensive narratives we collected about experiences of developing an age-friendly programme. The richness of the conversations demonstrates a rare opportunity for participants to reflect on their progress, given their busy operational roles in their organisations. Reflectivity is, as Mortari (2015: 1) argues, 'a very important mental activity, both in private and professional life', as it is a way of gaining meaning from the apparent unintelligibility of the real world. It is also a key element of experience-based learning for practitioners, especially where they can reflect upon activities such as the age-friendly programme. The accounts captured in these narratives were exceptionally detailed and, in most cases, reflected upon several years of work. The narratives provide a unique reconstruction of the evolution, development and implementation of the age-friendly model and the different stages that each locality had reached in its journey up to that point. What emerged from this research is the nuanced nature of each locality's analogous route to development and the complexity of the factors shaping its journey, which were not constant in time and space. Age-friendly development is not as linear and connected as it is envisaged as being in Figure 2.3. Instead, in these accounts, the journey towards age-friendliness was typically more of an evolutionary journey, with many twists and turns or roadblocks. In some cases, roadblocks were removed by enablers whilst in others, dead ends were reached, and lateral thinking took things in a different direction. The desire of age-friendly leaders to keep the agenda moving appears to be motivated by pragmatic social opportunism. The existing body of ageing-related work and their own knowledge base equipped many of the age-friendly leads, especially those in public-health or cognate areas, who had already developed the skills to understand the holistic nature and challenges of progressing this initiative.

DOI: 10.4324/9781003319801-5

The dimensions of re-creating places for ageing

Drawing upon the findings in Chapters 3 and 4, we have sought to synthe-
sise these into a model that identifies the key dimensions of how places
have been transformed and re-created in order for them to become more
age-friendly. Figure 5.1, which is based on these findings, shows four distinct quadrants, which are interconnected and affected by external factors.
Taking the top-left quadrant first, the *intervention* dimension reflects the
initial commitment process whereby localities decide to embark on the age-
friendly journey, whether for political or social motives. From an operational
perspective, three distinct strands then emerged: establishing the nature of
the age-friendly provision, what needed to be done and how to engage with
the community. This often involved auditing the suitability of the physical and social environment for age-friendliness, a process underpinned by
taking a clear advocacy role. To achieve that advocacy, collaboration and
the formation of partnerships within and across organisations were deemed
critical to getting the age-friendly message out. This stage also involved
reaching a broad range of stakeholders using a process of community public engagement with organisations to develop age-friendly objectives; this
could involve working on a one to one or a group basis. Moving to the top
right-hand quadrant, labelled *scale/place*, this represents the spatial setting
for communities, in which daily life takes place. The quadrant contains the
range of environments participants worked within, which comprise a continuum from city environments through to rural and coastal communities,
and sometimes a mixture of these community types. Accessibility emerged
as a key attribute in all communities, with much of the debate often con-
centrating on neighbourhoods at the micro scale. The spatial component
interconnects with the remaining two quadrants (*addressing barriers* and
inclusive design). *Addressing barriers* illustrates a key area of action, that
of identifying and addressing barriers in each of the age-friendly domains.
Communicating with older people and organisations is one way of over-
coming barriers and to maintain a dialogue on meeting older people's needs.
The final quadrant (*inclusive design*) highlighted the underlying principles
that environmental design needs to consider in re-creating age-friendly
environments which have broader benefits for all in existing and planned
developments.

But perhaps the one key factor that affects the entire age-friendly development process is the political climate, which impacts every quadrant in Figure 5.1 and runs along the two axes. The horizontal axis spans the national
level, as evidence from Canada, Ireland and the devolved governments (e.g.
Northern Ireland and Wales) demonstrates; in these locations, a national
strategy helps to prioritise the significance of ageing. It is also a priority

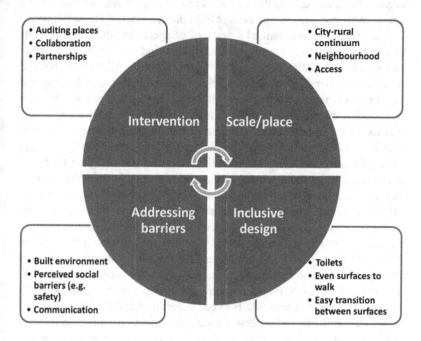

• Auditing places
• Collaboration
• Partnerships

• City-rural
  continuum
• Neighbourhood
• Access

Intervention   Scale/place

Addressing   Inclusive
barriers   design

• Built environment
• Perceived social
  barriers (e.g.
  safety)
• Communication

• Toilets
• Even surfaces to
  walk
• Easy transition
  between surfaces

Figure 5.1 Re-creating places and spaces: Age-friendly dimensions

for funding in these countries. Criticisms of the lack of a national ageing strategy in England to promote the age-friendly model are very pertinent and other bodies have highlighted the World Health Organization mantra of adding extra years to life and extra life to those years (Local Government Association 2013a), given the challenges and opportunities an ageing population poses for communities (Local Government Association 2015), and the opportunities for harnessing the visitor economy and local growth (Local Government Association 2013b), recognising the role of ageing consumers. Some interpretations point to the decisions by the UK government to focus its resources for ageing on dementia (Department of Health 2015; Connell et al. 2017; Connell and Page 2019a, 2019b), which we explore on pp. 138 and 140. The second axis running vertically was based on the characteristics of the locality, its leadership and its ability to leverage grants from national agencies and funding bodies (e.g. the Lottery Fund) with partners. The result is a continuum of age-friendly programmes that ranged from being entirely funded by a large grant on a limited-life basis to receiving no funding aside from that of officers' time or posts. Again, being able to partner both within organisations and externally with others to leverage funding advances the age-friendly mission, as was evident from the accounts of the participants.

Our research also identified a range of perspectives among participants about the distinctiveness of age-friendliness and dementia-friendliness. Some saw similarities between the two initiatives, whilst others pointed to dementia-friendly programmes being favoured in terms of funding and saw this as being to the detriment of the ageing agenda per se, although this funding stream had created a launchpad for age-friendly work in several localities. In other areas, it appeared to have created a degree of conflict between organisations as the project priorities and funding agendas of age-friendly and dementia-friendly initiatives were aligned to different outcomes. In some localities, this did not impede productive working relationships between a multitude of third-sector organisations, but, in others, resources and attention had been diverted away from a core focus on wider ageing issues to a narrower focus on dementia. Local charities helped with the development of the baseline work in the early stages of the age-friendly journey, as advocates of the age-friendly model and as a source of important volunteers in assisting with the programme of work. The external collaboration and goodwill built up within localities reflect the social capital and networks between different organisations, groups and individuals that can be harnessed, leveraging human resources in order to achieve age-friendly outcomes. This represents a critical component which is not easy to measure or evaluate. Participants described this as a hidden ingredient, one of the low-cost or no-cost innovations that they had identified and implemented. Even so, the absence of large pots of funding from a national source appears to be a major constraint on levelling up the existing programmes so as to reach a national benchmark of age-friendly provision in each of the domains.

Ageing, age-friendliness and levelling up

It is disappointing to see that the opportunity to address ageing as part of the government's levelling-up White Paper has been missed (UK Government 2022). Whilst this paper highlights national socio-geographic variations in life expectancy (as well as significant variations between neighbourhoods of towns, cities and rural areas of localities), it does nothing to address ageing explicitly, only including a few health-related interventions that will indirectly benefit those able to access them. Some analysts suggest that the UK is becoming a more divided nation after a period of levelling up that occurred under the Labour government of 1997–2010, and that this problem is especially acute for the ageing population (see Page and Connell 2022). The north–south gap in economic and social measures has been a constant element of the geography of the UK since the post-war period (although its origins were established during the UK's Industrial Revolution). It emerges most clearly in spatial variations in life expectancy. The nature of this gap was notably illustrated by Burton (2021: n.p.), who cites Office for National Statistics data:

> *between 2016 and 2018, Richmond-upon-Thames had the highest male healthy life expectancy at birth in the UK, at 71.9 years. This was 18.6 years longer than males in Blackpool, where it was only 53.3 years. In general, life expectancy at birth was highest in the four most southerly regions of England for both males and females. Much of this inequality was caused by higher mortality from heart and respiratory disease, and lung cancer in more deprived areas.*

Again, ageing is an invisible element of a major government strategy (apart from the example of levelling-up life expectancy) to transform the socio-economic geography of life in its levelling-up agenda. Caro and Morris (2002) argue that ageing is a national policy issue, but the implementation of policy solutions is largely delegated to local (or regional) government through funding and interventions. The UK's levelling-up agenda, which is premised on creating wealth by improving the economy and living environment, fails to recognise that by 2030, when many of its key performance indicators are due to report, the population structure will be different to the one on which policy decisions were based. Critics could use this to illustrate a continuum of interpretations, from seeing this as the continued neglect of ageing at a national level, to a more critical view that the report is age-blind, through to a perspective that this is deliberate ageism, whereby the skills and talents of the ageing population are ignored. This is ironic when we consider that the White Paper explicitly states:

> *But not everyone shares equally in the UK's success. While talent is spread equally across our country, the opportunity is not. Levelling up is a mission to challenge, and change, that unfairness. Levelling up means giving everyone the opportunity to flourish. It means people everywhere living longer and more fulfilling lives, and benefiting from sustained rises in living standards and well-being.* (UK Government 2022: 1)

The difficulty with such bland hyperbole is that for the lives of the older population to benefit from this strategy, the economy needs to prosper and for the benefits to trickle down to those localities that are most in need of growth. These spatial economic principles have created uneven geographies to date, and so they are unlikely to fundamentally change the socio-economic geography of the UK. For example, the White Paper identifies 20 towns where investment is planned, to help level up the geography of life chances. Yet the socio-economic disparities that exist nationally between north and south also exist on a local level, where they are equally challenging. Perhaps, however, this is viewed as being in the *too hard* basket and has been left to the local state to address, alongside the implications of an ageing demographic. That demographic is a reality today. Arguably, the agenda of addressing the internal disparities in localities is less headline-grabbing than some other political agendas but if it is attempted, it would help to break down some of the barriers facing the ageing population and enable them to fully participate in a civil society. Levelling up needs to occur locally if it is to achieve change in the social geography of inequality, especially in domains such as ageing. In the absence of levelling up, the age-friendly model, as Keyes and Benavides (2017) examine in the case of the USA, identifies the key role of political agents for change (e.g. elected officials; see Schneider, Teske and Mintrom 2011; Schneider and Teske 1992) at the local level, who directly age-friendly programme implementation (Mintrom 1997).

Why do some localities choose to become age-friendly whilst others do not?

The major unanswered question is *why do some localities embrace this innovative idea whilst others do not?* Whilst positive adoption factors exist, our study did not have the resources to also survey a selected sample of non-adopters to understand why these localities had not embraced the idea. Therefore, drawing upon our experience of working across dementia- and age-friendly initiatives, we can suggest several likely explanations that would be worthy of further investigation. Resource constraints (i.e. funding) are a likely determinant, as many local authorities have been looking to cut non-statutory roles to save money in response to a policy of austerity in public-sector finances. For this reason, they were unlikely to sign up for agendas when other operational needs had a claim upon resources. The absence of a champion to stimulate the process was also a critical determinant, along with supplementary factors such as the (in)visibility of ageing as a local issue; however, often the voluntary sector were strong advocates of the approach. In the UK example, the spatial concentration of exemplars of age-friendly practices in north-west England reflects the visionary outlook of political leaders and individuals within the local government structures in the region, who helped stimulate the creation of the 'age-friendly family'. That family is a growing phenomenon, as represented by the Centre for Ageing Better Community of Practice (COP). The example of how this COP had emerged as a response to perceived cuts in expenditure was also mentioned in other localities. The early work of the COP's age-friendly movement connected a growing number of localities to form an advocacy and knowledge-sharing network which sought to help disseminate good practice and increase understanding of the challenges and problems of developing age-friendly initiatives.

As the interviews with some of the leaders of the age-friendly developments in north-west England show, this initiative gathered momentum and spread to other local authority areas nearby, diffusing innovation to a broader north-west region and further afield to other northern towns. It is an impressive and energetic movement as the participants' openness, frankness and deep understanding of their localities are demonstrated in the vision and momentum behind the initiative. In contrast, other regions such as the east of England, the south coast of England (except Hastings, the Isle of White and Brighton), the Home Counties and the south-west (excluding Bristol and several other localities) have not embraced this movement. Yet as Keyes and Benavides (2017) admit, the existing theoretical frameworks used to understand and explain age-friendly adoption are still in need of further development. It is a little surprising to note the lack of resource sharing and cross-area territorial development of the age-friendly model among English local authorities outside of the north-west. Several joint age-friendly officers exist in smaller councils in Northern Ireland, which demonstrates one potential way for resource sharing to occur, given local authorities are now sharing administrative functions to achieve economies of scale. This approach may offer some scope for non-adopters seeking to develop this strand in future, but as yet the calls from bodies such as the Local Government Association (Local Government Association 2015) promoting the idea have not gathered momentum, even though other lobby groups, such as the Centre for Ageing Better (2022) continue to press organisations to adopt the age-friendly agenda locally and nationally.

The patchy geographical adoption of the age-friendly paradigm in the south and in south-west England may well be a function of the existence of prior agendas such as that around dementia, which charitable bodies have promoted with the establishment of dementia-friendly communities; this was given an impetus by the Prime Minister's Challenge (Department of Health 2015; Connell et al. 2017). This is most obvious in the case of London, which is now seeking simultaneously to be age-friendly and dementia-friendly, operating two agendas in parallel rather than in harmony. The city received a government grant to work with the Alzheimer's Society to promote the idea (see www.alzheimers.org.uk/get-involved/dementia-friendly-communities/london), yet the age-friendly concept still seems to be languishing and has seemingly been delegated to London boroughs; only three of the 33 boroughs currently progressing the idea, with Sutton featuring in a Local Government Association case study (see www.local. gov.uk/case-studies/sutton-our-plan-create-age-friendly-borough).   Creating competing agendas such as this reinvigorates the arguments on territoriality raised by our study's participants; and if the dementia-friendly approach is so similar to the age-friendly one, then surely a more collaborative process to combine the two agendas would avoid duplication of effort? As van Hoof et al. (2021: 19) argue, 'there is a strong need to link age-friendly work with existing urban policies and movements', such as dementia-friendliness and smart cities – especially given the growth in technological solutions for ageing, as well as agendas such as sustainability. In the case of dementia-friendly communities (DFCs), these are far more widespread than AFCs, and have a different grassroots model of development (see Connell and Page 2019b). With a few exceptions (where the age-friendly initiative sometimes emanated from the DFC), the gaps in age-friendly provision are marked by the existence of a DFC. To the outsider, it would appear that these communities have closed off the ageing issue, perhaps naively, by creating a DFC and so age-friendly is not seen to be needed. If that is the case, then the age-friendly agenda needs to be reinvigorated. These observations also highlight why a critique of the age-friendly model is, perhaps, long overdue.

Implications for age-friendly development: Critique of the age-friendly model

There have been numerous critiques of the way the concept of age-friendliness has been devised, adapted in different geographical contexts and then implemented. Steel (2015) surveyed the global models that have been developed (in parallel to the WHO age-friendly model), identifying several countries and/or city-based models (e.g. the WHO Active Ageing model, the New Zealand Positive Ageing model, the Social Connections Framework, the Healthy Ageing in Canada Framework, the Advantage Framework, the Conceptual Process framework and the Manchester Valuing Older People framework, which was superseded when the city joined the WHO age-friendly journey). What emerged from Steel's (2015) global review was a diverse range of terminology and backgrounds to these approaches to ageing. Steel (2015) reiterated the observations made in Chapter 2 about the highly descriptive nature of many academic studies of age-friendly programmes. However, Steel's, like many of the other recent studies, offers an opportunity to adopt a critical and reflective assessment of the age-friendly model through its inclusion of comments from the respondents' narratives. Among the key points are the following:

- As a concept, age-friendliness tends to be highly idealised (Plouffe, Kalache and Voelcker 2016) and perhaps it can never be fully achieved (see Scharlach 2016). The model is not easily replicated in every locality due to the nuances and idiosyncrasies of places and their populations as unique phenomena
- It is a developed-world phenomenon in the main, with limited application to the developing world because of the resources needed for its implementation, which are lacking in developing-world contexts; the model may need adapting for low-income countries
- Age-friendly activities are largely characterised by collaboration and their successful implementation requires a national policy and implementation strategy to make them a key priority for resourcing as well as to encourage their diffusion spatially
- Where national implementation is supported, it has been a local-authority-focused model of development, but the role of non-government organisations and voluntary bodies and community groups is vital to orientate age-friendliness towards a community model of development
- Steel (2015) highlighted the absence of documentation evaluating the effectiveness of the age-friendly approach in terms of achieving ageing-well objectives. The approach of the UK Government's (2022) levelling-up report, and its use of indicators to measure progress, is a much-needed simplification to help understand where the strengths, weaknesses, opportunities and threats exist for the age-friendly model in different localities
- The notion of levelling up is omitted from the WHO model and needs to be embraced at a locality level, so that any age-friendly programme recognises the existing social geography of the place where it is located and the inequalities therein, so these can be identified and prioritised for action. This is because the life experiences of older people, even in one locality, are extremely diverse and the age-friendly concept will only engage and work for those who can voice their opinions and can use the political system to pursue their agendas. Finding a conduit to the little-heard voices of older people, who may also be subject to inequality based on race, gender and income, is necessary. Otherwise the age-friendly agenda could become an exclusive development process that further perpetuates existing inequalities (Baars et al. 2016). As Yeh (2020) observed, being age-friendly does raise the spectre of focusing too much on one group, when things should be made better for

everyone. This reiterates some of the arguments advanced in Chapter 1 on creating people-friendly places and a more welcoming public realm for all

- The age-friendly model is not beginning from a blank sheet in most localities, as any analysis of community groups and clubs and societies for older people shows. Embracing the views of these more active citizens needs to be counterbalanced by listening to those people that other ageing strategies might wish to target in order to help overcome social isolation and barriers to participation, enabling these groups to access the local environment to enrich their daily lives. In conceptual terms, this might be about unlocking the potential of places that are typically within a 15-minute walk or journey time from the person's home, such as parks or open spaces; this may involve the implementation of accessibility measures, ensuring there are places to sit and addressing perceptions and the reality of safety and crime

- The age-friendly agenda focuses on one element of the life course (older age), whereas the narratives we have studied show that ageing is perceived differently by different people, although the term age-friendly sets out to offer everything to everyone. What has to be recognised, as some participants indicated, is that the 'ageing' category can span almost 50 years of calendar age, with people in that category having very different capabilities

- The age-friendly paradigm, from a theoretical perspective (see Joy 2021), is interpreted as a neo-liberalist response to short-term crises in the health and social care sector; its primary objective is to reduce the cost to the public sector and help people to live at home independently longer, so as to reduce the burden on the state. This interpretation can be applied to the levelling-up agenda (HM Government 2022) where the needs of the working-age population are prioritised as critical to generating economic prosperity; ageing people have to wait to see if they will be beneficiaries if that prosperity occurs and then trickles down to them indirectly. Poverty and financial precarity (Grenier et al. 2020) continue to be potential paths for people entering older age, and this will contribute to their potential exclusion from society

- Even where age-friendly programmes are put in place, they do not easily address systemic ageist attitudes in society at large, which significantly devalues their contribution, as the levelling-up agenda illustrates. In a neo-liberalist state, interventions are often justified on economic grounds when in fact there are other valid justifications. Enlightened interventions in age-friendly programmes like Safer at Home

programmes, for example, may not meet the neo-liberalist return-on-investment criteria but do fulfil a moral and social obligation to the older population
- Torku et al. (2021) points to the diversity of models in use for becoming age-friendly and points to two North American models that may be helpful for newcomers to the age-friendly family (Portland, Oregon and Quebec, Canada). However, establishing what makes a model successful led Torku et al. (2021) to question the basis upon which we assess the age-friendliness of communities. Currently, the principal tools used to evaluate the age-friendliness of localities are self-reporting surveys, verbal feedback and visual audits, all of which are associated with inherent methodological problems (e.g. they are very subjective and have limitations around recall and memory lapses). There is considerable scope to develop this area of evaluation work, given the development of psychological and physiological sensors that measure emotional responses and body functions to measure responses to the environment and activities
- There may be a greater role for objective indicators, as Davern et al. (2020) demonstrate, such as the use of spatial indicators implemented through the use of Geographical Information Systems technology to assess the lived environment of the eight WHO domains. In this way, seasonal variations in weather and climate can be better integrated alongside accessibility indicators and socio-economic variables to understand the local variations in issues in areas of multiple deprivation (also see Lowen et al. 2015)
- Evaluation tools tend to be very narrowly conceived, often associated with the public-health approach to assessing interventions; a whole-community approach to age-friendliness has yet to be developed for the majority of age-friendly programmes
- As Steel (2015) suggests, the WHO model does not recognise that age-friendly environments will be impacted by seasonal climatic variations; these need to be taken into account when assessing whether a service, product or location is age-friendly, as this may vary by season
- Rémillard-Boilard, Buffel and Phillipson (2021, cited in van Hoof et al. 2021: 20) pointed to four areas where age-friendly programmes need further enhancement:

First of all, the perception of older age needs to change. Second, key actors in age-friendly efforts need to be involved. Third, there is the need to respond to the (diverse) needs of older people. And fourth, the planning and delivery of age-friendly programmes need to be improved.

To assess progress in each of these areas, qualitative and quantitative data need to be collected. As Steel (2015: 50) aptly concluded:

> the WHO Global Network of Age-Friendly Cities and Communities has encouraged cities to adopt an age-friendly approach to urban interventions. However, to meet the challenges of ageing in the urban environment, it is important that policy-makers create supportive and enabling environments through interventions for their older population . . . age-friendly initiatives in the social and physical environment alongside multi-stakeholder collaborations are important factors that will help to build a mutually enhancing environment for older people.

This illustrates one additional strand of evidence in the narratives, namely the importance of providing support for older people as well as the enabling role of the age-friendly programme.

Creating a more sustainable future for age-friendly programmes

If the WHO model is idealistic, then many of the academic analyses of age-friendly as a paradigm have been characterised by a fundamental lack of understanding of the realities of developing and managing a complex multifaceted programme of work, and one that has, in the English context, been significantly underfunded. For example, van Hoof et al. (2021: 21) set out 10 steps to make communities age-friendly, very much in the same spirit of the WHO model, adopting a holistic view whereby all the domains are fully covered: for example, promotion of cross-sectorial collaboration; co-creation with target groups; retrofitting houses with affordable technology; understanding the friendly and unfriendly aspects of the built environment; strategies for improving route planning; making outdoor spaces accessible; provision of internet-accessible environments across the entire area to allow people to use apps to identify key facilities like toilets; involving citizens of all background to ensure their voices are heard; measuring the extent of age-friendliness in the communities, and future needs; and assessing existing age-friendly standards to ascertain whether they are outdated and if more agile approaches are needed. This list is overwhelming and certainly lies outside of the budgetary capabilities of many age-friendly programmes; it would need a long lead time to work through each of the items in a prioritised manner. Staff in the frontline managerial roles overseeing age-friendly programmes often have multiple tasks and priorities and so this academic analysis needs to congratulate many of the participants in this study, rather than criticise them for missing bits in the age-friendly jigsaw. Their major achievements amidst impossible competing demands, often with minimal resources, are impressive, as is their commitment and the can-do attitude of the age-friendly leads. If there had been any doubt, this study debunks any outdated thinking that public-sector employees are predominantly bureaucrats and not goal-oriented (Wright 2001). The narratives confirm the prevalence of traits such as caring and compassion among public servants (Willems 2020) who are passionate about what they do and proud of their many achievements in the age-friendly domain, or the activities they plan that will make a difference to people. This is one of the truly valuable elements of the qualitative research process, which enabled the highly engaged nature of the participants to emerge as a strong theme that unifies this group of people. The rich narratives leave an indelible impression of the participants' commitment to their aim of making a difference in people's lives.

The principal barriers which other interviews have identified in organisational research around ageing about dementia-friendly work (Connell and Page 2019a, 2019b) do not appear to be so obvious in the age-friendly setting, due to factors such as lateral thinking, political leverage, collaboration and networking to advance agendas. Nevertheless, there is certainly scope for these age-friendly programmes to leverage additional resources from newer agendas such as those concerned with climate change, energy efficiency and other linked agendas around sustainability. As Rosenbloom (2001) observed, the future mobility requirements of older people are likely to be more focused on car-driving, as the number of car owners has increased, and so shifting the mindset towards public transport use may be difficult even though a central tenet of many age-friendly schemes is the need to expand public transport usage among older people. A wide range of studies exist on the environmental design changes needed in our living environments to accommodate a growing ageing population (see Handler 2014), and as Grazuleviciute-Vileniske et al. (2020) highlight, this will involve the wider use of design concepts such as design for all, Universal Design and inclusive design, as well as more ecological and safe environments in the future. A key feature of these design principles, as Tao et al. (2021) observed, is the walkability of neighbourhoods in cities and access to key facilities, reiterating the comments of Participant 14 on the 15-minute city, which reduces the need for car use. In older urban environments this may involve retrofitting adaptations to ageing infrastructure, as Stagner et al. (2021) highlight. Other studies have also suggested (e.g. Coyle et al. 2021) that embedding the age-friendly approach in an institution's culture will have a spillover effect, as one behaviour change or innovation may impact another area of work. Coyle et al. (2021) pointed to three strategies used in Boston, USA to help with advocacy for age-friendliness. First, the spillover was reinforced by promoting the age-friendly initiative, which was accompanied by an anti-ageism campaign. Second, the achievements of the initiative were celebrated and publicised. Boston formed a combined age- and dementia-friendly business programme to make its services more age-inclusive. One consequence for the Main Street areas was that businesses requested that benches be placed outside their premises, and signage was improved by the Main Street organisation to aid wayfinding. Third, the programme 'made new friends but also kept [the] old ones' (Coyle et al. 2021), leveraging change and resources by connecting the programme's objectives with those of other organisations to create shared goals. The programme remained flexible to adapt to new agendas in Boston – such as anti-racism, prioritised by the City Mayor in 2020, extending the reach of the age-friendly message.

The future for ageing and age-friendly: Is '-friendly' a passing trend?

As a concept, age-friendliness has seen more than a decade of development in places and spaces. In one sense, the local state still provides a safety net for the aged citizen, through the social policies to which it adheres. Yet the deep meaning of *friendliness* is in danger of being diluted by the term *friendly*'s having become an in-vogue buzzword when used as an adjective with a hyphen (e.g. child-friendly, vegan-friendly, LBGTQ+-friendly, dog-friendly, dementia-friendly, among many other uses). Here the meaning and intent appear to be a wish to be seen as a welcoming environment for the specific group being targeted, and to say 'it is alright to visit or enter this area as it will meet your stated needs'. Its meaning also suggests a specific ideology that entails removing barriers through a process of making something or somewhere more 'friendly'. Other notions of friendliness may involve kindness, being helpful, warmth, respect, support, compassion and being welcoming, all of which will assist in breaking down barriers and some of the social isolation felt by older people in modern society. But operationalising this almost nebulous social construct means that much of the emphasis has been on accessibility and physical access, as the more emotive aspects, associated with feelings of place, attachment and belonging, are more complex and less easy to achieve in a predominantly ageist society. In addition, with so many 'friendly' causes competing for airtime and resources, the significance of 'age-friendly' is in danger of being watered down, with the term reduced to the status of another sticker in a shop window or a logo on a website. For the age-friendly agenda to be taken seriously and to get the attention it deserves, it needs to have a powerful narrative and story attached to it that has a strong emotional attachment, so that it can be differentiated from other 'friendly' agendas.

From a public-policy perspective, ageing is not going to diminish in significance, even if there is a national policy vacuum currently in the UK. It will continue to bubble away and manifest itself in the local state, not least due to the many crises associated with ageing and service delivery (e.g. bed-blocking due to a crisis in social care and inadequate capacity to deal with the volume of demand), alongside a growing demand for independent-living assistance. The partnerships that coalesce in many age-friendly pro-grammes between the local state and voluntary sector, often providing mutual aid to citizens, are elevated to a much higher level of awareness in policy circles by the age-friendly movement, which delivers practical age-friendly targeted help.

Building the infrastructure and attitudinal changes needed to embed a more positive outlook towards ageing people is very much a long-term objective that needs to span all aspects of society. The only time this seems to become real for the public is when the issues associated with ageing are articulated through the voices of family members, illustrating the potential emotional power of ageing as a phenomenon about ageing well. Unless there is a fundamental shift in political thinking that radically realigns age-ing to a mainstream government agenda in the UK at a national level, the age-friendly paradigm is going to remain a highly localised scheme with a wide range of shared experiences of successes and failures. Yet if we are indeed to become a more 'friendly' society with all these new uses of the adjective, we need to develop a better public awareness of how age-friendly intersects with these other agendas. Ageing needs to be a positive feature of our society, and one which has the same degree of political support that other protected attributes (e.g. race, sex, disability) have received before the ageing crisis reaches unmanageable proportions.

References

Age Friendly Bristol. (2019). *Make Your Business More Age-Friendly*. Bristol: Age Friendly Bristol. agefriendlybristol.org

Age Friendly Ireland. (2021). *Ten Universal Design Features to Include in a Lifetime Adaptable and Age Friendly Home*. Navan: Age Friendly Ireland. https://agefriendlyireland.ie/wp-content/uploads/2021/10/AFI-10-Universal-Design-Features.pdf.

Age UK. (2019). *Later Life in the United Kingdom 2019*. London: Age UK. www.ageuk.org.uk/globalassets/age-uk/documents/reports-and-publications/later_life_uk_factsheet.pdf

Almeida, M. (2016). Age-friendly walkable urban spaces: A participatory assessment tool. *Journal of Housing for the Elderly*, 30(4): 396–411.

Anon. (2022). Age Scotland calls for urgent action to meet needs of ageing population. *Scottish Housing News*, 13 January 2022, www.scottishhousingnews.com/articles/age-scotland-scotland-must-rise-to-meet-the-needs-of-an-ageing-population.

Arnold, E. and Boggs, K. (2019). *Interpersonal Relationships E-Book: Professional Communication Skills for Nurses*. Oxford: Elsevier Health Sciences.

Arnstein, S. (1969). A ladder of citizen participation. *Journal of the American Institute of Planners*, 35(4): 216–24.

Audit Commission. (2008). *Don't Stop Me Now: Preparing for an Ageing Population*. London: Audit Commission.

Baars, J., Dannefer, D., Phillipson, C. and Walker, A. (eds.) (2016). *Aging, Globalization and Inequality: The New Critical Gerontology*. London: Routledge.

Barclays. (2015). *An Ageing Population: The Untapped Potential for Hospitality and Leisure Businesses*. London: Barclays.

Bartlett, A., Frew, C. and Gilroy, J. (2012). *Understanding Material Deprivation among Older People*. In-House Research 14. London: Department for Work and Pensions.

Baskaran, H. (2020). *Celebrating Active Ageing*. Chennai: Notion Press.

Bass, B. (1990). *Bass & Stogdill's Handbook of Leadership*. New York: Free Press.

Beard, S. (2022). *Age Friendly: Ending Ageism in America*. Boca Raton, FL: Routledge.

Bhuyan, M., Lane, A., Moogoor, A., Močnik, Š. and Yuen, B. (2020). Meaning of age-friendly neighbourhood: An exploratory study with older adults and key informants in Singapore. *Cities*, 107: 102940.

Bichard, J.-A. and Knight, G. (2011). *Publicly Accessible Toilets: An Inclusive Design Guide*. London: Royal College of Art.

Biggs, S. and Carr, A. (2015). Age- and child-friendly cities and the promise of intergenerational space. *Journal of Social Work Practice*, 29(1): 99–112.

Blakie, A. (1999). *Ageing and Popular Culture*. Cambridge: Cambridge University Press.

Booth, C. (1889). *Life and Labour of the People in London*. London: Macmillan.

Booth, C. (1894). *The Aged Poor in England and Wales*. London: Macmillan and Co.

Boulton-Lewis, G. and Tam, M. (eds.) (2011). *Active Ageing, Active Learning*. Dordrecht: Springer.

Boyer, G. R. and Schmidle, T. P. (2009). Poverty among the elderly in late Victorian England 1. *The Economic History Review*, 62(2): 249–78.

Bryman, A. (2008). *Social Research Methods*. 3rd Edition. New York: Oxford University Press.

Buffel, T., Handler, S. and Phillipson, C. (eds.) (2018). *Age-Friendly Cities and Communities: A Global Perspective*. Bristol: Policy Press.

Buffel, T., McGarry, P., Phillipson, C., De Donder, L., Dury, S., De Witte, N., Smetcoren, A. and Verté, D. (2019). Developing age-friendly cities: Case studies from Brussels and Manchester and implications for policy and practice. In F. Caro and K. Fitzgerald (eds.), *International Perspectives on Age-Friendly Cities* (pp. 27–45). London: Routledge.

Buffel, T. and Phillipson, C. (2016). Can global cities be 'age-friendly cities'? Urban development and ageing populations. *Cities*, 55: 94–100.

Buffel, T. and Phillipson, C. (2018). A manifesto for the age-friendly movement: Developing a new urban agenda. *Journal of Aging & Social Policy*, 30(2): 173–92.

Buffel, T., Phillipson, C. and Scharf, T. (2012). Ageing in urban environments: Developing 'age-friendly' cities. *Critical Social Policy*, 32(4): 597–617.

Burton, K. (2021). A country divided: Why England's North–South divide is getting worse. *Geographical*, 5 May 2021, https://geographical.co.uk/uk/item/3906-a-country-divided-why-england-s-north-south-divide-is-getting-worse.

Butler, R. (2006). Ageism. In R. Schulz (ed.), *The Encyclopedia of Ageing A–K* (pp. 41–2). New York: Springer.

Cacioppo, J. and Patrick, W. (2008). *Loneliness: Human Nature and the Need for Social Connection*. New York: W.W. Norton.

Caro, F. and Fitzgerald, K. (eds.) (2018). *International Perspectives on Age-Friendly Cities*. London: Routledge.

Caro, F. and Morris, R. (2002). Devolution and aging policy. *Journal of Aging & Social Policy*, 14(3–4): 1–14.

Centre for Ageing Better (2022). *The State of Ageing 2022*. London: Centre for Ageing Better.

Centre for Cities. (2019). A decade of austerity. London: Centre for Cities, www.centreforcities.org/reader/cities-outlook-2019/a-decade-of-austerity/

Chao, T-Y. (2018). *Planning for Greying Cities: Age-Friendly City Planning and Design Research and Practice*. London: Routledge.

Charmaz, K. (2003). Grounded theory: Objectivist and constructivist methods. In N. Denzin and Y Lincoln (eds.), *Strategies for Qualitative Inquiry* (pp. 249–91). 2nd Edition. Thousand Oaks, CA: SAGE.

City of Unley. (2019). *Age Friendly Checklist*, https://extranet.who.int/agefriendly world/26530-2/.

Clifford, D. (2016). Charitable organisations, the great recession and the age of austerity: Longitudinal evidence for England and Wales. *Journal of Social Policy*, 46(1): 1–30.

Cohen, W. and Levinthal, D. (1990). Absorptive capacity: A new perspective on learning and innovation. *Administrative Science Quarterly*, 35: 128–52.

Connell, J. and Page, S. J. (2019a). An exploratory study of creating dementia-friendly businesses in the visitor economy: Evidence from the UK. *Heliyon*, 5(4):e01471.

Connell, J. and Page, S. J. (2019b). Destination readiness for dementia-friendly visitor experiences: A scoping study. *Tourism Management*, 70: 29–41.

Connell, J., Page, S. J., Sheriff, I. and Hibbert, J. (2017). Business engagement in a civil society: Transitioning towards a dementia-friendly visitor economy. *Tourism Management*, 61: 110–28.

Corden, A. and Sainsbury, R. (2006). *Using Verbatim Quotations in Reporting Qualitative Social Research: Researchers' Views*. York: Social Policy Research Unit Report, University of York.

Coyle, C., Gleason, S. and Mutchler, J. (2021). Spillover benefits and achieving sustainability of age-friendly communities. *The Gerontologist*, 62(1): 29–35.

Craig, G., Mayo, M., Popple, K., Shaw, M. and Taylor, M. (eds.) (2011). *The Community Development Reader: History, Themes and Issues*. Bristol: Policy Press.

Creswell, J. and Poth, C. (2013). *Qualitative Inquiry and Research Design: Choosing Among Five Approaches*. 4th Edition. London: SAGE Publications.

Cropley, D. (2016). Measuring capacity for innovation in local government organizations. *Innovation*, 2(1): 31–45.

Cunha, M., Clegg, S. and Mendonça, S. (2010). On serendipity and organizing. *European Management Journal*, 28(5): 319–30.

Danziger, J.(1978). *Making Budgets: Public Resource Allocation*. London: SAGE.

Davern, M., Winterton, R., Brasher, K. and Woolcock, G. (2020). How can the lived environment support healthy ageing? A spatial indicators framework for the assessment of age-friendly communities. *International Journal of Environmental Research and Public Health*, 17(20): 7685.

DEFRA (Department for Food and Rural Affairs). (2021). *Statistical Digest of Rural England Population*. https://assets.publishing.service.gov.uk/government/uploads/system/uploads/attachment_data/file/1028819/Rural_population__Oct_2021.pdf

de Mello, L. (2021). Population ageing and local governments: Does engagement with the local community change over the lifecycle? *Local Government Studies*, 47(3):364–85.

Department for Business, Energy and Industrial Strategy. (2017). *Building our Industrial Strategy*. https://assets.publishing.service.gov.uk/government/uploads/system/uploads/attachment_data/file/664563/industrial-strategy-white-paper-web-ready-version.pdf.

Department of Health. (2015). *Prime Minister's Challenge on Dementia 2020*. London: Department of Health.

de Widt, D. (2021). The impact of demographic trends on local government financial reserves: evidence from England. *Local Government Studies*, 47(3): 405–28.

Dollery, B. and Wallis, J. (2001). *The Political Economy of Local Government*. Cheltenham: Edward Elgar.

Everingham, J., Warburton, J., Cuthill, M. and Bartlett, H. (2012). Collaborative governance of ageing: Challenges for local government in partnering with the seniors' sector. *Local Government Studies*, 38(2): 161–81.

Eversley, J. (2019). *Social and Community Development: An Introduction*. London: Red Globe Press.

Federal/Provincial/Territorial Ministers Responsible for Seniors. (2007). *Age-Friendly Rural and Remote Communities: A Guide*. Ottawa: Ministry of Industry.

Firmstone, J. and Coleman, S. (2015). Public engagement in local government: The voice and influence of citizens in online communicative spaces. *Information, Communication & Society*, 18(6): 680–95.

Fisher, F. (2007). The twelve competencies: Leadership training for local government officials. *National Civic Review*, 96(2): 28–36.

Fitzgerald, K. and Caro, F. (2014). An overview of age-friendly cities and communities around the world. *Journal of Aging & Social Policy*, 26(1–2): 1–18.

Fitzgerald, K. and Caro, F. (eds). (2018). *International Perspectives on Age-Friendly Cities*. London: Routledge.

Flynn, N. (2012). *Public Sector Management*. 6th Edition. London: SAGE.

Formosa, M. (ed.) (2019). *The University of the Third Age and Active Ageing: European and Asian-Pacific Perspectives*. Cham: Springer Nature.

Frizzell, N. (2019). Wee demand action! What can we do about Britain's public toilet shortage? *The Guardian*, 15 January 2019.

Garfinkel, H. (1967). *Studies in Ethnomethodology*. Englewood Cliffs, NJ: Prentice Hall.

Gargan, J. (1981). Consideration of local government capacity. *Public Administration Review*, 41(6): 649–58.

Garon, S., Paris, M., Beaulieu, M., Veil, A. and Laliberte, A. (2014). Collaborative partnership in age-friendly cities: Two case studies from Quebec, Canada. *Journal of Aging & Social Policy*, 26: 73–87.

Getha-Taylor, H., and Morse, R. S. (2013) Collaborative leadership development for local government officials: Exploring competencies and program impact. *Public Administration Quarterly*, 37(1): 71–102.

Gibney, S., Zhang, M. and Brennan, C. (2020). Age-friendly environments and psychosocial wellbeing: A study of older urban residents in Ireland. *Aging and Mental Health*, 24(12): 2022–33.

Giddens, A. (1998). *The Third Way: The Renewal of Social Democracy*. Cambridge: Polity.

Gilchrist, A. and Taylor, M. (2011). *The Short Guide to Community Development*. 2nd Edition. Bristol: Policy Press.

Gilroy, R. (2005). Meeting the information needs of older people: A challenge for local governance. *Local Government Studies*, 31(1): 39–51.

Glasgow City Council (2015). *Age-Friendly Glasgow*. Glasgow: Glasgow City Council.

Goldman, L., Owusu, S., Smith, C., Martens, D. and Lynch, M. (2016). Age-friendly New York City: A case study. In T. Moulaert and S. Garon (eds.), *Age-Friendly Cities and Communities in International Comparison: Political Lessons, Scientific Avenues, and Democratic Issues* (pp. 171–90). Cham: Springer International Publishing.

Government Office for Science. (2019). *Future of an Ageing Population*. London: Government Office for Science.

Gray, J., Kaslow, N. and Allbaugh, L. (2020). Introduction to the special issue: Advocacy in public service settings. *Psychological Services*, 17(S1): 1–4.

Grazuleviciute-Vileniske, I., Seduikyte, L., Teixeira-Gomes, A., Mendes, A., Borodinecs, A. and Buzinskaite, D. (2020). Aging, living environment, and sustainability: What should be taken into account? *Sustainability*, 12(5): 1853.

Greenstein, L., Abraham, A. and Tipping, B. (2019). Treating complexity in the older adult – The role of the geriatric giants. *South African Family Practice*, 61(6). doi: https://doi.org/10.4102/safp.v61i6.5065.

Grenier, A., Hatzifilalithis, S., Laliberte-Rudman, D., Kobayashi, K., Marier, P. and Phillipson, C. (2020). Precarity and aging: A scoping review. *The Gerontologist*, 60(8): e620–e632.

Hajnal, Z. and Trounstine, J. (2010)Who or what governs? The effects of economics, politics, institutions, and needs on local spending. *American Politics Research*, 38(6): 1130–63.

Handler, S. (2014). *An Alternative Age-Friendly Handbook: Featuring New & Emerging Age-Inclusive Initiatives with Additional Reflections (& Provocations) on Ageing in the Contemporary City*. Manchester: University of Manchester Library.

Harper, S. (2006). *Ageing Societies*. London: Hodder Education.

Harper, S. (2020). The COVID-19 pandemic and older adults: Institutionalised ageism or pragmatic policy? *Journal of Population Ageing*, 13(4): 419–25.

Hartley, J. (2005). Innovation in governance and public services: Past and present. *Public Money and Management*, 25(1):27–34.

Harvey, D. (2003). The right to the city. *International Journal of Urban and Regional Research*, 27(4): 939–41.

Hendriks, A.-M., Jansen, M., Gubbels, J., De Vries, N., Molleman, G. and Kremers, S. (2015). Local government officials' views on intersectoral collaboration within their organization: A qualitative exploration. *Health Policy and Technology*, 4(1): 47–57.

Hepple, L. (2001). Multiple regression and spatial policy analysis: George Udny Yule and the origins of statistical social science. *Environment and Planning D: Society and Space*, 19(4): 385–407.

Hobhouse, L. (1911). *Liberalism*. London: Williams and Norgate.

Hobsbawm, E. (2010). *The Age of Revolution 1789–1848*. London: Phoenix Press.

Hofäker, D., Hess, M. and König, S. (eds.) (2016). *Delaying Retirement: Progress and Challenges of Active Ageing in Europe, the United States and Japan*. Singapore: Palgrave Macmillan.

Hofmann, S., Räckers, M., Beverungen, D. and Becker, J. (2013). Old blunders in new media? How local governments communicate with citizens in online social networks. Paper presented at the 2013 46th Hawaii International Conference on System Sciences.

Hollway, W. and Jefferson, T. (2012). *Doing Qualitative Research Differently: A Psychosocial Approach*. Los Angeles: SAGE Publications.

Hood, R., Goldacre, A., Abbott, S. and Jones, R. (2022). Patterns of demand and provision in English adult social care services. *British Journal of Social Work*. In press.

House of Lords (2012). *Ready for Ageing. Report of Sessions 2012–13*. House of Lords: HMSO.

Howaldt, J., Oeij, P., Dhondt, S. and Fruytier, B. (2016). Workplace innovation and social innovation: An introduction. *World Review of Entrepreneurship, Management and Sustainable Development*, 12(1): 1–12.

Hysing, E. (2014). How public officials gain policy influence: Lessons from local government in Sweden. *International Journal of Public Administration*, 37(2): 129–39.

Inman, P. (2021). Austerity is alive and well, and giving public services a kicking. *The Guardian*, 27 February 2021.

Jacobs, J. (1961). *The Death and Life of Great American Cities*. New York: Random House.

James, N. and Busher, H. (2009). *Online Interviewing*. London: SAGE.

Jehu, L., Visram, S., Marks, L., Hunter, D. J., Davis, H., Mason, A., Liu, D. and Smithson, J. (2018). Directors of public health as 'a protected species': Qualitative study of the changing role of public health professionals in England following the 2013 reforms. *Journal of Public Health*, 40(3):e203–e210.

Jenkins, L., Bramwell, D., Coleman, A., Gadsby, E., Peckham, S., Perkins, N. and Segar, J. (2016). Integration, influence and change in public health: Findings from a survey of Directors of Public Health in England. *Journal of Public Health*, 38(3):e201–e208.

Johns, M. (2020). *10 Years of Austerity*. London: Institute for Public Policy Research.

Jones, R. (2007). A journey through the years: Ageing and social care. *Ageing Horizons* 6: 42–51.

Joy, M. (2018). Problematizing the age friendly cities and communities program in Toronto. *Journal of Aging Studies*, 47: 49–56.

Joy, M. (2021). Neoliberal rationality and the age-friendly cities and communities program: Reflections on the Toronto case. *Cities*, 108:102982.

Kavšek, M., Rogelj, V. and Bogataj, D. (2021). Smart age-friendly environments. *IFAC-PapersOnLine*, 54(13): 768–73.

Kelley, J., Dannefer, D. and Al Masarweh, L. (2019). Addressing erasure, microfication and social change: Age-friendly initiatives and environmental gerontology in the 21st century. In T. Buffel, S. Handler, and C. Phillipson (eds.), *Age-Friendly Cities and Communities: A Global Perspective* (pp. 51–72). Bristol: Policy Press.

Kenny, S., McGrath, B. and Phillips, R. (eds.) (2017). *The Routledge Handbook of Community Development: Perspectives from Around the Globe.* London: Routledge.

Keyes, L. and Benavides, A. (2017). Local government adoption of age friendly policies: an integrated model of responsiveness, multi-level governance and public entrepreneurship theories. *Public Administration Quarterly*, 41(1), 149–85.

King, A., King, D., Banchoff, A., Solomonov, S., Ben Natan, O., Hua, J., Gardiner, P., Rosas, L. G., Rodriguez Espinosa, P., Winter, S. J., Sheats, J., Salvo, D., Aguilar-Farias, N., Stathi, A., Hino, A. A. and Porter, M. M. (2020). Employing participatory citizen science methods to promote age-friendly environments worldwide. *International Journal of Environmental Research and Public Health*, 17(5): 1541.

Lefebvre, H. (1968). *Le Droit à la Ville.* Paris: Anthropos.

Lefebvre, H. (1976). *The Survival of Capitalism.* Trans. Frank Bryant. London: Allison and Busby. (Originally published 1973 as *La survie du capitalisme*)

Lefebvre, H. (1991). *The Production of Space.* Trans. Donald Nicholson-Smith. Oxford: Basil Blackwell.

Lehning, A. J. (2012). City governments and aging in place: Community design, transportation and housing innovation adoption. *The Gerontologist*, 52(3): 345–56.

Lewin, K. (1935). *A Dynamic Theory of Personality: Selected Papers.* New York: McGraw Hill.

Local Government Association (2013a). *Adding Extra Years to Life and Extra Life to Those Years: Local Government Guide to Healthy Ageing.* London: Local Government Association.

Local Government Association (2013b). *The Visitor Economy: A Potential Powerhouse of Local Growth.* London: Local Government Association.

Local Government Association (2015). *Ageing: The Silver Lining: The Opportunities and Challenges of an Ageing Society for Local Government.* London: Local Government Association.

Lofland, J., Snow, D., Anderson, L. and Lofland, L. (2006). *Analyzing Social Settings: A Guide to Qualitative Observation and Analysis.* 4th Edition. Belmont, CA: Wadsworth/Thomson Learning.

Lowen, T., Davern, M., Mavoa, S. and Brasher, K. (2015). Age-friendly cities and communities: Access to services for older people. *Australian Planner*, 52(4): 255–65.

Marmot, M., Goldblatt, P., Boyce, T., McNeish, D., Grady, M. and Geddes, I. (2010). *Fair Society Healthy Lives* (The Marmot Review). www.instituteofhealthequity.org/resources-reports/fair-society-healthy-lives-the-marmot-review.

McCrillis, E., Skinner, M. and Colibaba, A. (2021). Developing rural insights for building age-friendly communities. *Journal of Rural Studies*, 81: 336–44.

McDonald, B., Scharf, T. and Walsh, K. (2018). Creating an age-friendly county in Ireland: Stakeholders' perspectives on implementation. In T. Buffel, S. Handler and C. Phillipson (eds.), *Age-Friendly Cities and Communities: A Global Perspective* (pp. 143–66). Bristol, Policy Press.

McGarry, P. (2019). Developing age-friendly policies for cities: Strategies, challenges and reflections. In T. Buffel, T., S. Handler, S. and C. Phillipson (eds.), *Age-Friendly Cities and Communities: A Global Perspective* (pp. 231–50). Bristol: Policy Press.

McGarry, P. and Morris, J. (2011). A great place to grow old: A case study of how Manchester is developing an age-friendly city. *Working with Older People* 15(1): 38–46.

Menec, V. and Brown, C. (2018). Facilitators and barriers to becoming age-friendly: A review. *Journal of Aging & Social Policy*, 1–23.

Menec, V., Means, R., Keating, N., Parkhurst, G. and Eales, J. (2011). Conceptualizing age-friendly communities. *Canadian Journal on Aging/La revue canadienne du vieillissement*, 30(3): 479–93.

Menec, V., Hutton, L., Newall, N., Nowicki, S., Spina, J. and Veselyuk, D. (2013). How 'age-friendly' are rural communities and what community characteristics are related to age-friendliness? The case of rural Manitoba, Canada. *Ageing & Society*, 35: 203–23.

Menec, V., Newall, N., Milgrom, R. and Camps, D. (2021). Exploring the sustainability of age-friendly initiatives in a Canadian province. *The Gerontologist*, 62(1): 18–28.

Menec, V., Novek, S., Veselyuk, D. and McArthur, J. (2014). Lessons learned from a Canadian province-wide age-friendly initiative: The Age-Friendly Manitoba Initiative. *Journal of Aging and Social Policy*, 26: 33–51.

Menec, V. H. (2017). Conceptualizing social connectivity in the context of age-friendly communities. *Journal of Housing For the Elderly*, 31(2): 99–116.

Michels, A. and De Graaf, L. (2010). Examining citizen participation: Local participatory policy making and democracy. *Local Government Studies*, 36(4): 477–91.

Michels, A. and De Graaf, L. (2017). Examining citizen participation: Local participatory policymaking and democracy revisited. *Local Government Studies*, 43(6): 875–81.

Mintrom, M. (1997). Policy entrepreneurs and the diffusion of innovation. *American Journal of Political Science,* 41(3): 738–70.

Mortari, L. (2015). Reflectivity in research practice: An overview of different perspectives. *International Journal of Qualitative Methods*, 14(5): 1–9.

Moulaert, T. and Garon, S. (eds.) (2015). *Age Friendly Cities and Communities in International Comparison. Political Lessons, Scientific Avenues, and Democratic Issues*. Cham: Springer.

Mowat, C. (1957). Charity and casework in Late Victorian London: The work of the Charity Organisation Society. *Social Service Review, 31*(3), 258–70.

Mowat, C. (1961). *The Charity Organisation Society, 1869–1913: Its Ideas and Work*. London: Methuen.

Murray, K., Roux, D., Nel, J., Driver, A. and Freimund, W. (2011). Absorptive capacity as a guiding concept for effective public sector management and conservation of freshwater ecosystems. *Environmental Management*, 47(5): 917–25.

Murtagh, B., Cleland, C., Ferguson, S., Ellis, G., Hunter, R., Rodriguez Añez, C. R., Becker, L. A., Ferreira Hino, A. A. and Reis, R. S. (2022). Age-friendly cities, knowledge and urban restructuring. *International Planning Studies*, 27(1): 62–76.

Nabatchi, T., and Amsler, L. (2014). Direct public engagement in local government. *The American Review of Public Administration*, 44(4_suppl.): 63S–88S.

Neal, M., DeLaTorre, A. and Carder, P. (2014). Age-friendly Portland: A university city-community partnership. *Journal of Aging & Social Policy*, 26(1–2): 88–101.

Nykiforuk, C., Rawson, D., McGetrick, J. and Belon, A. (2017). Canadian policy perspectives on promoting physical activity across age-friendly communities: Lessons for advocacy and action. *Ageing and Society*, 39(2): 307–39.

O'Mahoney, J. and Vincent, S. (2014). Critical realism as an empirical project: A beginner's guide, in P. Edwards, J. O'Mahoney and S. Vincent (eds.), *Studying Organisations using Critical Realism: A Practical Guide* (pp. 1–20). Oxford: Oxford University Press.

Ospina, S. and Dodge, J. (2005). It's about time: Catching method up to meaning – the usefulness of narrative inquiry in public administration research. *Public Administration Review*, 65(2): 143–57.

Page, S. J. (1987). A new source for the historian of urban poverty: A note on the use of charity records in Leicester 1904–29. *Urban History Yearbook*, 14: 51–60.

Page, S. J. (1988). *Poverty in Leicester 1881–1911: A Geographical Perspective*, unpublished Ph.D. thesis, Department of Geography, University of Leicester.

Page, S. J. and Connell, J. (2022). *Ageing and the Visitor Economy*. London: Routledge.

Page, S. J. and Hardyman, R. (1996). Place marketing and town centre management: A new tool for urban revitalization. *Cities*, 13(3): 153–64.

Parasuraman, A., Ziethmal, A. and Berry, L. (1985). A conceptual model of service quality and its implications for further research. *Journal of Marketing* 48: 41–50.

Park, R., Burgess, E. and McKenzie, R. (1925). *The City*. Chicago: University of Chicago Press.

Paschen, J.-A. and Ison, R. (2014). Narrative research in climate change adaptation – Exploring a complementary paradigm for research and governance. *Research Policy*, 43(6): 1083–92.

Patterson, I. (2018). *Tourism and Leisure Behaviour in an Ageing World*. Wallingford: CABI.

Peng, S. and Maing, M. (2021). Influential factors of age-friendly neighborhood open space under high-density high-rise housing context in hot weather: A case study of public housing in Hong Kong. *Cities*, 115:103231.

Phillips, R. and Pittman, R. (eds.) (2009). *An Introduction to Community Development*. London: Routledge.

Plouffe, L. and Kalache, A. (2011). Making communities age friendly: State and municipal initiatives in Canada and other countries. *Gaceta Sanitaria*, 25: 131–37.

Plouffe, L., Garon, S., Brownoff, J., Foucault, M-L., Lawrence, R., Beaupre, J-P. and Toews, V. (2013). Advancing age-friendly communities in Canada. *Canadian Review of Social Policy*, 68/69: 24–38.

Plouffe, L., Kalache, A. and Voelcker, I. (2016). A critical review of the WHO age-friendly cities methodology and its implementation. In T. Garon and S. Mouleart (eds.), *Age-Friendly Cities and Communities in International Comparison: Political Lessons, Scientific Avenues, and Democratic Issues* (pp. 19–36). Cham: Springer.

Pollitt, C. (2010). Envisioning public administration as a scholarly field in 2020. *Public Administration Review* (December Special Issue): S292–S294.

Porter, M. and Kramer, M. (2011). Creating shared value. *Harvard Business Review* (Jan.–Feb.): 1–17.

Powell, D. (1996). *The Edwardian Crisis: Britain 1901–14*. London: Bloomsbury Publishing.

Prendergast, D. and Garattini, C. (eds.) (2015). *Aging and the Digital Life Course*. Oxford: Berghahn Books.

Public Health Agency of Canada (2012). *Age Friendly Communities in Canada: Community Implementation Guide*. Hc-sc.gc.ca.

Public Health England. (2019). *PHE Strategy 2020–25*. London: Public Health England.

Public Health England. (2021). *Wider Impacts of COVID-19 on Physical Activity, Deconditioning and Falls in Older Adults*. London: Public Health England.

Quadango, J. (2007). *Ageing and the Life Course: An Introduction to Social Gerontology*. 4th Edition. New York: McGraw Hill.

Ravi, K., Fields, N. and Dabelko-Schoeny, H. (2021). Outdoor spaces and buildings, transportation, and environmental justice: A qualitative interpretive meta-synthesis of two age-friendly domains. *Journal of Transport & Health*, 20: 100977.

Rawls, J. (1971). *A Theory of Justice*. Cambridge, MA: Belknap Press.

Raymond, A., Bazeer, N., Barclay, C., Krelle, H., Idriss, O., Tallack, C., and Kelly, E. (2021). *Our Ageing Population: How Ageing Affects Health and Care Need In England*. London: The Health Foundation.

Rémillard-Boilard, S. (2018). The UK network of age-friendly communities: A general review. *Working with Older People*, 22(1): 30–8.

Rémillard-Boilard, S. (2019). The development of age-friendly cities and communities. In T. Buffel, S. Handler and C. Phillipson (eds.), *Age-Friendly Cities and Communities: A Global Perspective* (pp. 13–32). Bristol: Policy Press.

Rémillard-Boilard, S., Buffel, T. and Phillipson, C. (2021). Developing age-friendly cities and communities: Eleven case studies from around the world. *International Journal of Environmental Research and Public Health*, 18(1): 133.

Reuter, A., Liddle, J. and Scharf, T. (2020). Digitalising the age-friendly city: Insights from participatory action research. *International Journal of Environmental Research and Public Health*, 17(21): 1–17.

Richter, M. (1964). *The Politics of Conscience: T. H. Green and His Age*. London: Weidenfeld & Nicolson.

Ritch, A. (2012). History of geriatric medicine: From Hippocrates to Marjory Warren. *Journal of the Royal College of Physicians Edinburgh*, 42(4), 368–74.

Riva, G., Marsan, A. and Grassi, C. (eds) (2014). *Active Ageing and Healthy Living*. Amsterdam: IOS Press.

Rose, M. (ed.) (1985). *The Poor and the City: The English Poor Law and Its Urban Context 1834–1914*. Leicester: Leicester University Press.

Rosenbloom, S. (2001). Sustainability and automobility among the elderly: An international assessment. *Transportation*, 28(4): 375–408.

Rowe, J. and Kahn, R. (1987). Human aging: Usual and successful. *Science* 237: 143–9.

Rowntree, S. (1901). *Poverty: A Study of Town Life*. London: Macmillan and Co.

Royal Commission on the Aged Poor. (1898). *Report of the Royal Commission on the Aged Poor, appointed to consider whether any alterations in the system of Poor Law Relief are desirable, in the case of persons whose destitution is occasioned by incapacity for work resulting from old age, or whether assistance could otherwise be afforded in those cases*. London: HMSO.

Russell, E., Skinner, M. and Colibaba, A. (2021). Developing rural insights for building age-friendly communities. *Journal of Rural Studies*, 81: 336–44.

Russell, E., Skinner, M. and Fowler, K. (2019). Emergent challenges and opportunities to sustaining age-friendly initiatives: Qualitative findings from a Canadian age-friendly funding program. *Journal of Aging & Social Policy*, 1–20.

Salingaros, N. (2021). Modernist architecture melts our brains. *The Critic*, 4 September, https://thecritic.co.uk/modernist-architecture-melts-our-brains/.

Salmons, J. (2011). *Cases in Online Interview Research*. London: SAGE.

Samuel, L. (2021). *Age-Friendly: Ending Ageism in America*. London: Routledge.

Sánchez-González, D., Rojo-Pérez, F., Rodríguez-Rodríguez, V. and Fernández-Mayoralas, G. (2020). Environmental and psychosocial interventions in age-friendly communities and active ageing: A systematic review. *International Journal of Environmental Research and Public Health*, 17(22):1–35.

Sanders, K. and Canel, M. J. (2015). Mind the gap: Local government communication strategies and Spanish citizens' perceptions of their cities. *Public Relations Review*, 41(5): 777–84.

Saner, E. (2021). The urinary leash: How the death of public toilets traps and trammels us all. *The Guardian*, 1 December 2021.

Scharlach, A. (2012). Creating age-friendly communities in the United States. *Ageing International*, 37:25–38.

Scharlach, A. (2016). Age-friendly cities: For whom? By whom? For what purpose? In T. Moulaert and S. Garon (eds.), *Age-Friendly Cities and Communities in International Comparison: International Perspectives on Aging* (pp. 305–30). Cham: Springer.

Scharlach, A. and Lehning, A. (2016). *Creating Aging-Friendly Communities*. Oxford: Oxford University Press.

Scheidt, B. and Schwarz, R. (eds.) (2013). *Environmental Gerontology: What Now?* London: Routledge.

Schneider, M. and Teske, P. (1992). Toward a theory of the political entrepreneur: Evidence from local government. *American Political Science Review*, 86(3): 737–47.

Schneider, M., Teske, P. and Mintrom, M. (2011). *Public Entrepreneurs*. Princeton, NJ: Princeton University Press.

Scott, M. (2021). Planning for age-friendly cities. *Planning Theory & Practice*, 22(3): 457–492.

Sennett, R. (2018). *Building and Dwelling: Ethics for the City*. London: Allen Lane.

Shannon, L. (2018). *Local Government as a Local Service Provider: A Case Study of Ireland's Age-Friendly Cities and Counties Programme. Local Government Research Series 14*. Dublin: Institute of Public Administration.

Shock, N. (1952). *Trends in Gerontology*. Stanford: Stanford University Press.

Silverman, D. (ed.) (2016). *Qualitative Research*. London: SAGE.

Simhony, A. (2005). A liberalism of the common good: Some recent studies of T. H. Green's moral and political theory. *The British Journal of Politics and International Relations*, 7(1): 126–44.

Smiles, S. (1859). *Self-Help: With Illustrations of Character and Conduct*. London: John Murray.

Soja, E. (2013). *Seeking Spatial Justice*. Minnesota: University of Minnesota Press.

Stafford, P. (ed.) (2019). *The Global Age-Friendly Community Movement: A Critical Appraisal*. Oxford: Berghahn.

Stagner, J., Ting, D., Abdallah, Y., Al-Kodmany, K., Baker, J. A., Balo, F., . . . Estévez, A. (2021). *Sustainable Engineering for Life Tomorrow*. London: Lexington Books.

Standards Research (2019). *A Canadian Roadmap for an Ageing Society*. Canadian Standards Association. www.csagroup.org

Stedman-Jones, G. (1971). *Outcast London: A Study in the Relationship Between Classes in Victorian Society*. Oxford: Clarendon Press.

Steel, S. (2015). Key characteristics of age-friendly cities and communities: A review. *Cities*, 47: 45–52.

Stephenson, A. (2013). *The Public Sector: Managing the Unmanageable*. London: Kogan Page.

Stroud, D. and Walker, K. (2012). *Marketing to the Ageing Consumer: The Secrets to Building an Age-Friendly Business*. Basingstoke: Palgrave Macmillan.

Sun Life. (2020). Retiring ageism. https://www.sunlife.co.uk/over-50-life-insurance/over-50-data-centre/ageism/

Svara, J. (1985). Dichotomy and duality: Reconceptualizing the relationship between policy and administration in council-manager cities. *Public Administration Review*, 45(1): 221–32.

Svensson, G. and Wood, G. (2005). The serendipity of leadership effectiveness in management and business practices. *Management Decision*, 43(7/8): 1001–9.

Swift, H. and Steeden, B. (2020). *Doddery But Dear: Examining Age-Related Stereotypes*. London: Centre for Ageing Better.

Tao, Y., Zhang, W., Gou, Z., Jiang, B. and Qi, Y. (2021). Planning walkable neighborhoods for 'Aging in Place': Lessons from five aging-friendly districts in Singapore. *Sustainability*, 13(4): 1742.

Thane, P. (ed.) (1978). *The Origins of British Social Policy*. London: Croom Helm.

Thane, P. (1989). History and the sociology of ageing. *Social History of Medicine*, 2(1): 93–6.

The Joseph Rowntree Foundation Task Group on Housing, Money and Care for Older People (2004). *From Welfare to Well-Being – Planning for an Ageing Society.* York: Joseph Rowntree Foundation.

Thompson, M. (2021). What's so new about New Municipalism? *Progress in Human Geography*, 45(2): 317–42.

Thomson, D. (1984). The decline of social welfare: Falling state support for the elderly since early Victorian times. *Ageing and Society*, 4(4): 429–49.

Timonen, V. (2016). *Beyond Successful and Active Ageing: A Theory of Model Ageing.* Bristol: Policy Press.

Titmuss, R. (1951). Social administration in a changing society. *The British Journal of Sociology*, 2(3): 183–97.

Tibbalds, F. (2001). *Making People-Friendly Towns: Improving the Public Environment in Towns and Cities.* London: Routledge.

Tinker, A. and Ginn, J. (2015). *An Age Friendly City: How Far Has London Come?* London: King's College London.

Torku, A., Chan, A. and Yung, E. (2021). Age-friendly cities and communities: A review and future directions. *Ageing and Society*, 41(10): 2242–79.

Townsend, P. (1981). The structured dependency of the elderly: A creation of social policy in the twentieth century. *Ageing and Society* 1(1): 5–28.

Turner, N. and Cannon, S. (2018). Aligning age-friendly and dementia-friendly communities in the UK. *Working with Older People*, 22(1): 9–19.

UK Government. (2022). *Levelling Up the United Kingdom: Summary.* www.gov.uk/government/publications/levelling-up-the-united-kingdom

United Nations. (1955). *Social Progress Through Community Development.* New York: United Nations.

United Nations Department of Economic and Social Affairs. (2019). *World Population Ageing 2019.* www.un.org/en/development/desa/population/publications/pdf/ageing/WorldPopulationAgeing2019-Report.pdf.

van Hoof, J. and Marston, H. (2021). Age-friendly cities and communities: State of the Art and future perspectives. *International Journal of Environmental Research and Public Health*, 18(4): 1644.

van Hoof, J., Marston, H., Brittain, K. and Barrie, H. (2019). Creating age-friendly communities: Housing and technology. *Healthcare*, 7(4): 130.

van Hoof, J., Marston, H., Kazak, J. and Buffel, T. (2021). Ten questions concerning age-friendly cities and communities and the built environment. *Building and Environment*, 199:107922.

van Hoof, J., van den Hoven, R., Hess, M., van Staalduinen, W., Hulsebosch-Janssen, L. and Dikken, J. (2022). How older people experience the age-friendliness of The Hague: A quantitative study. *Cities*, 124:103568.

Wahl, H.-W., and Weisman, G. D. (2003). Environmental gerontology at the beginning of the new millennium: Reflections on its historical, empirical, and theoretical development. *The Gerontologist*, 43(5): 616–27.

Walker, A. (1980). The social creation of poverty and dependency in old age. *Journal of Social Policy*, 9(1): 49.

Walker, A. (1981). Towards a political economy of old age. *Ageing and Society*, 1(1): 73–94.

Walker, A. (2015). The concept of active ageing. In A. Walker and C. Aspalter (eds.), *Active Ageing in Asia* (14–29). London: Routledge.

Walker, A. (2017). Why the UK needs a social policy on ageing. *Journal of Social Policy*, 47(2): 253–73.

Walker, A. (ed.) (2018). *The Future of Ageing in Europe*. Singapore: Palgrave Macmillan.

Walker, A. and Aspalter, C. (eds.) (2015). *Active Ageing in Asia*. London: Routledge.

Walker, A. and Foster, L. (2014). *The Political Economy of Ageing and Later Life*. Cheltenham: Edward Elgar Publishing.

Walker, R. (2006). Innovation type and diffusion: An empirical analysis of local government. *Public Administration*, 84(2): 311–35.

Walmsley, D. and Jenkins, J. (1992). Tourism cognitive mapping of unfamiliar environments. *Annals of Tourism Research*, 19(3): 268–86.

Warner, M. and Zhang, X. (2021). Serving an ageing population: Collaboration is key. *Local Government Studies*, 47(3): 498–517.

Webster, L. and Mertova, P. (2007). *Using Narrative Inquiry as a Research Method*. London: Routledge.

Welsh Government (2021). *Age-Friendly Wales: Our Strategy for an Ageing Society*. https://gov.wales/age-friendly-wales-our-strategy-ageing-society-html

Whitaker, B. and Browne, K. (1971). *Parks for People*. London: Schocken Books.

White, M. and Verdusco, L. (2018). Communicating with older adults. *Home Healthcare Now*, 36(3): 181–4.

WHO (World Health Organization). (1994). *Health for All*. Geneva: World Health Organization.

WHO (World Health Organization). (2002). *Active Ageing: Policy Framework*. Geneva: World Health Organization.

WHO (World Health Organization). (2007a). *Age Friendly Cities Guide*. Geneva: World Health Organization.

WHO (World Health Organization). (2007b). *WHO Age-Friendly Cities Project Methodology: Vancouver Protocol*. Geneva: World Health Organization.

WHO (World Health Organization). (2015). *Measuring the Age-Friendliness of Cities: A Guide to Using Core Indicators*. Geneva: World Health Organization.

Willems, J. (2020). Public servant stereotypes: It is not (at) all about being lazy, greedy and corrupt. *Public Administration*, 98(4): 807–23.

Willmott, M., Womack, J., Hollingworth, W. and Campbell, R. (2016). Making the case for investment in public health: Experiences of Directors of Public Health in English local government. *Journal of Public Health*, 38(2): 237–42.

Woo, J.-M. and Choi, M. (2020). Why and how have Korean cities embraced the World Health Organization's Age-Friendly Cities and Communities model? *Journal of Aging & Social Policy*, 1–18.

Woo, J.-M. and Choi, M. (2022). Why and how have Korean cities embraced the World Health Organization's Age-Friendly Cities and Communities model? *Journal of Aging & Social Policy*, 34(2): 293–310.

Wright, B. (2001). Public-sector work motivation: A review of the current literature and a revised conceptual model. *Journal of Public Administration Research and Theory*, 11(4): 559–86.

Xiang, L., Shen, G., Tan, Y. and Liu, X. (2021). Emerging evolution trends of studies on age-friendly cities and communities: A scientometric review. *Ageing and Society*, 41(12): 2814–44.

Yeh, J. (2020). A critical review of the WHO Age-Friendly Cities methodology and implementation. Unpublished Ph.D., University of California, San Francisco.

Yule, G. (1899). An investigation into the causes of changes in pauperism in England, chiefly during the last two intercensal decades (Part I). *Journal of the Royal Statistical Society*, 62(2): 249–95.

Zaidi, A., Harper, S., Howse, K., Lamura, G. and Perek-Bialas, J. (eds.) (2018). *Building Evidence for Active Ageing Policies*. Singapore: Palgrave Macmillan.

Index

Note: Information in figures and tables is indicated by page numbers in **bold** and *italic*.

166 *Index*

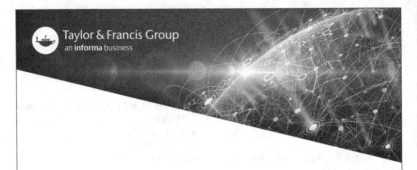

Printed in the United States
by Baker & Taylor Publisher Services